The nation of New Zealand has long been an inspiration and blessing to me since my first visit with Darlene in 1963. It is a prophetic nation. The people of God have profoundly ministered into YWAM. Since 1967, when YWAM NZ was launched, some of our best YWAM International leaders have come from this land. Included among them are David and Susan Cole.

In the opening days of 2000, I traveled and met with leaders and congregations from Kaitaia to Invercargill, from Chatham Islands to New Plymouth. I began to sense God would not only minister to a new youthful generation of Kiwis but release revelation that would guide Impact World Tour in many nations. This book chronicles the battles and victories but reveals the principles and God's responses that make it all possible. Abram needed Melchizedek to enter the land of the Philistines, Paul needed Lydia to enter Philippi, Jesus said to the seventy in Luke 10, look for the "man of peace" in each place you go. The Word also says, "honor to whom honor is due." The "gateway principle" of going to the elders of the host people—the Maori elders, the city elders, and the Christian elders—is revelation to be used in evangelizing nations and places around the world. On behalf of Christians everywhere, thank you Kiwi Christian leaders for leading out once again. Thank you Mark Anderson, John Dawson, and so many others for leading and setting an example, and modeling how to touch a new generation nationwide. Thank you David and Susan Cole for the godly leaders you are, and for giving us all this wonderful record of a movement under God's hand in New Zealand.

Loren Cunningham
Founder, Youth With A Mission

Prior to embarking on the IWT project, David received a clear, unmistakable word that "a great and effectual door is now opened to him" (1 Corinthians 16:9).

IWT is the manifestation of this door opening, birthed by the Holy Spirit, to take cities and nations, beginning with their Jerusalem—New Zealand (Acts 1:8).

The evangelistic and discipleship process undergirding IWT has been the key mandate from our Lord Jesus Christ. This model integrates the work and ministry of the churches, kingdom companies, and marketplace ministries for the end-time harvest.

What is being told in this book is the substance and evidence of things to come for global evangelism before Christ's return.

Khoo Oon Theam
President and CEO, OTI Consulting
Singapore

Impact World Tour has successfully undertaken the most comprehensive evangelistic mission in the whole of our nation's history. This has lifted the place of campaign evangelism to a new place of acceptance. The number of people who have been won to Christ the last few weeks even exceeds the wonderful ministry of the Billy Graham Crusades of 1959 in New Zealand. I believe we need to recognize that God has done something special and has introduced a new revival level in soul winning.

I commend this book and thank David and Susan Cole for recounting in a most readable style the God-given vision and the blessings and challenges of the mission that followed.

This book is unintentionally about servant leadership. It should be helpful for all to observe and learn how God fulfilled His purposes through the servant leadership of David Cole.

Rev. Hon. Graeme Lee, MNZM, JP.
Former Minister of Internal Affairs
New Zealand

IMPACT WORLD TOUR

the New ZEALAND STORY

David and SUSAN COLE

YWAM PUBLISHING
P.O. Box 55787 Seattle, WA 98155

YWAM Publishing is the publishing ministry of Youth With A Mission. Youth With A Mission (YWAM) is an international missionary organization of Christians from many denominations dedicated to presenting Jesus Christ to this generation. To this end, YWAM has focused its efforts in three main areas: (1) training and equipping believers for their part in fulfilling the Great Commission (Matthew 28:19), (2) personal evangelism, and (3) mercy ministry (medical and relief work).

For a free catalog of books and materials, contact

YWAM Publishing
P.O. Box 55787, Seattle, WA 98155
(425) 771-1153 or (800) 922-2143
www.ywampublishing.com

Impact World Tour: The New Zealand Story

10 09 08 07 06 10 9 8 7 6 5 4 3 2 1

Published by YWAM Publishing
P.O. Box 55787
Seattle, WA 98155

ISBN 978-1-57658-408-8

Printed in the United States of America.

Acknowledgments

With thanks

To all those who contributed to this manuscript, especially Lexie Waters, Grace Farag and Jo Osborne for their work during the tour. Thanks Jackie Sheppard, June Dooney, Lisa Orvost and Ross Tooley for your immense contributions in the outcome of this book.

Photographs

Thanks to Nathan Golden, Jo Martin and Marty Melville for capturing highlights of the tour through their camera lenses and for allowing us to use their photographs.

Dedication

In recording the story of Impact World Tour, it has been impossible to acknowledge or even begin to do justice to the thousands of people who worked tirelessly without recognition to impact their communities with the Gospel. We can only name a small representative sample of the thousands of wonderful saints who spent long hours making IWT happen in their communities. We are so grateful for all your work.

The Lord is not so unjust as to forget your work and labour of love which you have shown toward His name (Hebrews 6:10)

We dedicate this book to all who have laboured.

Foreword

During the past few weeks I have traveled through Australia and Fiji, visiting local Christians that are preparing for the Impact World Tour evangelistic events in their towns and cities. Excitement is high and in some places the harvest has already begun. In one town I visited, most of the young men in a juvenile correctional facility responded to the gospel during the preliminary visit of an IWT evangelist, Maori strongman, Jason Hotere.

Coordinators from YWAM campaigns have been placed in towns months in advance and local networks are beginning to form. I found myself surrounded by pastors, prayer leaders, business people, educators and youth leaders, all eager for stories of what had happened in other lands and advice about how to prepare for the dramatic days ahead.

In each case I found myself longing for a copy of this book. The story of the NZ campaign is a remarkable one and David and Sue Cole have been able to record so much that is helpful to the next generation of campaigns.

At first glance an IWT team coming to your nation may be perceived as a spectacular evangelistic event. In reality, God is up to much more than that. In New Zealand the tour fit within the long story of restoration and revival that is the multi-generational task of the body of Christ. This nation wide campaign was a catalyst for the unity of the church and the integration of Christians laboring in all the arenas of society.

Imagine Indigenous Moari leadership, business and media executives, educators and government people as well as pastors and youth workers, all working together to serve the new generation. Imagine hip hop, indigenous dance and extreme sports exploding into the Youth culture of your town. Imagine stadium events with world class performers en masse. Imagine people from some of the hardest subcultures in your city responding to Jesus in thousands.

If you want more than an inspiring story. If you want to see the principles of harvest and transformation lived out then this text is your companion, handbook and personal guide.

John Dawson
President. YWAM International

Contents

Chapter One

Arise, Shine; For Your Light Has Come!

January 21, 2004

Hellooooooo, Gisborne!" boomed the big man's voice over the microphone. The excited crowd replied with shouts, whistles, and yahoos. "I didn't hear you! Make some noise for Team Xtreme International!"

The big men smashed piles of concrete blocks, bent steel bars, and tore up telephone books as the crowd cheered them on. The raw power of the feats of the strong men and their stories of the power of Christ to transform their lives held large numbers of children, youth, and families spellbound.

Impact World Tour 2004 was under way in New Zealand, commencing in the small, most eastern city of the world, Gisborne. Any doubts and fears I had experienced during the three-year buildup to the tour soon dissipated. Months of preparation culminated here.

Then Jason Hotere, a big Maori TX member, walked over to an old gray car, rubbed his hands together, took some deep breaths, and strained almost every muscle in his body to flip the car over. It finally capitulated. While still recovering his breath, his body glistening with sweat, Jason went on to share that just as he could flip the car over, God can turn our lives upside down. We may be in the driver's seat, but God wants to take control of our lives. While he told the gospel story, the crowd was attentive. He did not seem to be "preaching to the crowd" but rather telling the story of God's love for each individual. He demonstrated the story of creation by kneeling down and drawing a male and female figure, then blowing into the microphone to demonstrate God's giving them breath. The memory of the concrete walls breaking was a strong reminder of the heartache of separation God felt from His creation as we willfully disregarded Him. Then Jason gave the appeal for all those who wanted Jesus to take control of their lives and to have the walls of sin broken down through the death of Jesus.

From all over the stadium, people surged forward in response. As I watched a long-haired young man determinedly walk forward, I was reminded of my own journey of faith that began almost three decades earlier. So much had happened since the time I first became a Christian. Now I was part of a mission to impact the youth of New Zealand with the gospel message that had changed my life forever.

Although my loving, disciplined parents were faithful churchgoers, in my late teens I decided that church was not relevant to my life. In 1976, with my auburn hair reaching halfway down my back, I dropped out of university. Living in a decked out VW van, my friend Brian and I worked the best surf spots in the nation, taking casual jobs when we needed money. Despite my rejection of the church, a spiritual hunger began to gnaw inside me. While we tried out some outstanding surf in New Zealand, I also tried different ways to satisfy my growing spiritual appetite. Meditation, vegetarianism, and New Age theories fascinated me for a while, but they gave me no lasting satisfaction.

While I surfed daily, I also continued my spiritual quest in earnest. In Christchurch, the largest city in the South Island, I stayed for some months in a house with some friends. One day two huge Maori ex-gang members came around on their motorbikes, answering an advertisement for a VW van motor we needed to sell. As I opened the door for them, I felt very small in comparison to their huge frames. Both were clad in black leather jackets. One had shoulder-length dreadlocks. They seemed friendly enough.

"Heh, man, whatcha reading?" asked the one with the dreadlocks.

I held up my book on Eastern mysticism, still guarded in my response to these visitors.

"You need to read the Bible. That sort of stuff will bend your mind."

The Bible! That was the last thing I expected him to say.

While buying the VW motor, he shared parts of his story. Life had been a struggle for survival in his family consumed by alcohol and violence. He joined a gang, was heavily involved in drugs, and ended up in jail. His life turned upside down when he eventually became a follower of Jesus.

"You should try Him, bro." Then, shifting his gaze from the book still lying on the table to eyeball me directly, he added, "Nothing else will satisfy you." I felt uncomfortable under the scrutiny of his gaze.

This was one of several encounters I had had with people we called "Jesus freaks." I couldn't help but notice the presence and peace of these followers of Jesus. I was just too proud to acknowledge that I didn't have the same peace they had.

Later that year I traveled to the northern part of New Zealand and settled in the city of Whangarei. I rented a small sleep-out behind a stucco house on the outskirts of the city.

A young woman with long sandy hair who lived in the house adjoining the sleep-out took time to befriend me. "So, what do you think life is really all about, Dave?" she asked one day. I looked from the garden of the stucco house to the surrounding native bush area. Months of carefree surfing and searching in different spiritual directions had brought me to one conclusion: I said that we all needed to find God. "It doesn't matter which path we take to find Him, though," I was quick to add. Even as I started talking about my theories of spiritual reality, my voice sounded hollow. In a moment of honesty, my voice trailed off, "I really don't know for sure."

This young woman did not argue with me or criticize me. She merely smiled, flicked her long hair over her shoulder, and said, "I have some books on spiritual truth you might be interested in reading. Feel free to borrow them."

Satan is Alive and Well on Planet Earth by Hal Lindsay grabbed my attention. As the candlelight cast a flickering glow in the sleep-out, the truths in this book began to come alive to me. I read how Satan blinds the minds of people through deception of other religions, immorality, and drugs and that none of us measures up to God's standard. As I thought about the book, I became aware of my own shortcomings and the emptiness of my life without God. I understood for the first time who Jesus really was, and that through His death on the cross I could experience His forgiveness and life with Him forever. That candlelit room became a haven of peace as I knelt and asked God's forgiveness for the way I had lived. I felt a burden lift. I began to daily experience the power and presence of God in a personal way. It was one month before my twenty-first birthday.

I immediately understood the dreadlock gang member's instruction to read the Bible. I quickly developed an insatiable appetite for reading, memorizing, and meditating on the Scriptures. I told everyone I met, perhaps with more zeal than wisdom, about the importance of following Jesus. No one had instructed me to do these things.

I returned to university in Christchurch with the conviction that I needed to complete the horticultural course I had begun. After my studies, I continued to grow in my newfound faith and to pray about my future. Months later, I heard a quiet inner voice address me. "Dave, I want to train you for world evangelism in the last days." I had never heard a voice like it before. It was quiet, deeply personal, authoritative, resonating in my own spirit and causing a depth of response. Was this a directive coming from God Himself? Was He, in that brief interaction, outlining the main purpose for my life?

Later, while discussing my future with a friend, I referred to this. "World evangelism," he mused. "Somehow, Dave, I cannot imagine you as a traditional church minister! Have you heard of Youth With A Mission or YWAM (pronounced *why-wham*)? They have a training program for young people who want challenge, adventure, and involvement in evangelism. You may be interested. I'm going to Auckland and will bring you back a brochure."

The Discipleship Training School I attended in September proved to be all my friend said it would be. Men and women of faith who had experience across the globe taught us each week. They lived what they preached. God was taking me to a new depth in understanding of who He really is and revealing His purpose for my life.

I saw a quality of Christianity I had not encountered before and was deeply challenged to walk a life of faith, giving up everything for Jesus.

We joined with hundreds of Australian young people on the beaches of Sydney for part of our three-month field assignment. One day as the leader of a team of thirty participants, I needed to make sure they were paired up for the afternoon's outreach. One blonde student had no partner for the afternoon. "You can come with me if you like," I offered casually. "What's your name?"

"Sue." My mind was focused on the afternoon's evangelism.

As the hot Australian sun beat down on us, I put aside my desire to surf. I could tell Sue meant business with God as we prayed together for the afternoon. Her prayer was earnest and compassionate as she asked the Lord to lead us to the right people and touch their hearts as we shared the reality of God's love with them.

We approached two bronzed surfers, packing away their gear.

"Hi, guys. Mind if we talk to you for a while?" I asked.

Very quickly we were engaged in conversation, and I found they were living a similar lifestyle to what I had when surfing around New Zealand. It was easy to share with them how I had become a believer. The surfers were in no hurry to leave as we talked about Christ's death and resurrection.

Finally, sensing their attentiveness, I challenged them. "So what is it that stops you from becoming followers of Jesus?"

After a moment's thought, one said, "I couldn't give up my lifestyle."

"Same," said the other.

"Can we pray for you, then?" asked Sue. She was not giving up easily!

The afternoon raced by as we shared with other beachgoers—a family, a girl who had just gone through a painful relationship breakup, a lonely young man. I admired the way Sue spoke words of encouragement and comfort. As I heard snippets of her story, I wanted to know more about this young

Australian woman. All too soon, however, we had to report back with the rest of our team.

Oh well, Lord, that's the sort of girl I could be interested in, I thought. Before I knew it, I was back in Auckland, and I had entirely dismissed any thoughts of Sue.

After further training with YWAM, I found myself leading an evangelism team to Queenstown in the South Island of New Zealand. Queenstown was breathtaking in its beauty. Even in 1979 it was one of the most popular tourist resorts in New Zealand. We rented a small three-bedroom house on the lakefront, tucked away at the foot of the Remarkable Mountains, for the token sum of one dollar per year. A steady flow of backpackers found their way to our home, joining other travelers we met in the streets. Mirroring the way I had come to Christ two years before, many travelers also came to know the Lord through the ministry of the YWAM team.

When a busload of weary Australian YWAMers pulled into our driveway at the beginning of 1980, I leapt aboard to share with them accommodation details during their stay. Over one hundred and twenty young people had gathered in Queenstown for three weeks of intensive training and evangelism.

"Does everyone have somewhere to stay for the night?" I asked, after reading the logistical detail. As I took note of several hands, I was surprised to see a familiar face at the back of the bus. It was Sue! *What was she doing here?*

"What are you doing here?" I asked, hoping I did not sound as surprised as I felt. "I thought you were still studying in Australia."

"It's good to see you, Dave," she replied. Then she continued pensively, "I finished my degree in dentistry this year and was offered an excellent job. However, I heard that YWAM was holding a three-week outreach in New Zealand and felt

I was to come, even though it precluded me from the job. So here I am!"

It was one of the best outreaches I had ever been part of. Daily, we saw people come to Christ. Days were long and hard, but exhilarating. I found myself increasingly attracted to Sue as I observed her wholehearted enjoyment of the outreach also.

One day on the steps of our lakefront home, she began to tell me how the Lord was leading her to stay on in New Zealand. "I'll have to return briefly to Australia at the end of the outreach," she said. Then, looking more intently at me she added, "After all, I only came for three weeks!"

Just then a young man interrupted us. I watched Sue walk toward the lakefront out of the corner of my eye, noticing afresh how attractive she was. Again I wanted to spend more time with her.

So God was speaking to her about staying in NZ. Was this coincidental, or could this girl be my future marriage partner? YWAM had a policy of no romantic relationships during outreaches, to which I adhered. As the outreach finished, however, I did not want Sue to return to Australia without discovering if there was more than just attraction involved.

Taking a deep breath, I asked if I could meet her before she left the following morning. Was it my imagination, or was her "of course" tinged with the same enthusiasm I felt?

The moon shimmered on the still water as we made our way around the lakefront. I decided to come straight to the point. "Sue," I began, hesitating slightly, trying to put into words the stirring I felt in my heart toward her, "I don't want to waste your time or mine, or the Lord's for that matter, but I have been attracted to you. I've been wondering what is going on."

Hardly a romantic start. My mouth felt dry.

Smiling, she took my hand. "Dave," she said, "I've been feeling the same. To be honest, seeking a relationship was the last thing I thought about in coming to New Zealand. I was involved in a close friendship with a young man in Australia."

(I took note of the *was*.)

"Although we were suited in so many ways, we both came to realize that marriage was not part of God's highest plan for us. That happened just before I came over here. So I was almost avoiding you at first."

"Almost?" I asked.

"Well," Sue continued, "until that day when we were talking together on the steps of the house by the lake. You later came and apologized, as someone had interrupted that conversation. I figured you were more interested in me than you were letting on."

Help, I thought. *What do I do now?* I sensed that God had called me to a life of leadership, of missionary service, and of pioneering. While I desired a life partner to share that, I knew that not everyone was suited to that lifestyle. I had asked the Lord many times for a wife who was prepared to go anywhere and do anything.

We backtracked and marveled over the growing mutual attraction we had had toward each other and some of the similar plans and dreams we held for the future. As I looked up at the majestic mountains silhouetted in the moonlight, I felt the peace of God envelop me. I said, "Let's trust our whole situation and friendship to the Lord and ask Him to show us about any future involvement during these ten days you will be in Australia." Sue left for Melbourne the following morning, and while I completed the outreach details, I counted the days until her return.

When I met her at the airport, I knew I wanted to spend my life with this young woman. Two weeks before we were married, in March 1980, we received a strong prophetic word that summed up the main theme of our life together. "*You shall be combine harvesters together, and you shall have many children."*

"What did you think of that, Dave?" Sue asked afterward.

"Well, combine harvesters are efficient, massive machines, reaping and threshing vast quantities of grain at the same time. Our current method of one-to-one evangelism is like harvesting manually. Maybe in the future God has some sort of larger scale evangelism for us."

"What about the many children?" she asked with a grin.

"Well," I said, "we'll handle that as they come, one at a time!"

Over the next twenty years, we moved many times around New Zealand as we gained experience in different aspects of ministry. We eventually relocated in Singapore, in 1994, fulfilling our long-term desire to live in Asia. After we adjusted to the dense urban sprawl and high-rise living of city life, Singapore soon became home for us. The two youngest of our six children were born there.

My role as the YWAM Regional Director for South East Asia and Australia involved much travel into the surrounding countries, particularly Malaysia, Indonesia, and Brunei. I thrived on the challenge and opportunities to share the gospel and help pioneer many new works in these parts of Asia.

The sickly sweet smell of the busy night markets in Kuala Lumpur wafted through the warm air. As I wandered past the stalls, a thin Asian man sitting cross-legged on a mat in front of some baskets caught my attention.

"Do you know Jesus?" I asked. He looked at me blankly.

"Jesus Christ, Son of God," I said, more slowly.

"Don't know," he said in broken English. I shut out the sound of the people milling around and knelt beside him. This young man, who I guessed was in his mid-twenties, had never heard the name Jesus. I took time to explain the gospel to him. He was one of the millions on our back doorstep who had never heard the gospel.

Indonesia was experiencing much turmoil during this period. Many Christians were martyred during political and religious conflicts, like fifteen-year-old Roy, the eldest son of one of our YWAM families, who was ruthlessly killed for refusing to deny his faith.

Despite persecution and martyrdom, the YWAM work flourished in Indonesia. With simple faith and very little material possessions, these young leaders inspired me as they gave their all. They established orphanages, agricultural programs, and other community-development projects, as well as teaching English. At the same time, they shared the gospel. What a privilege it was to serve alongside these leaders!

Although I was deeply fulfilled in the work in South East Asia, and I had always been involved either directly or indirectly in evangelism, I could hardly describe our effectiveness as that of "combine harvesters." Occasionally I wondered if the word that Sue and I had received before we were married about combine harvesters would ever be realized. I thought our six children certainly fulfilled the "many children" part of that word!

Since the start of the twenty-first century, both Sue and I had felt a vague stirring toward change. Over the years, I had come to recognize this as the Lord's preparation of our hearts toward a new venture. Nevertheless, I felt our family would be based in the thriving hub of Singapore for a long time.

I could never have imagined that a telephone call would herald the beginning of a new endeavor. It would also shift us into a new dimension of evangelism.

Chapter Two

Ask of Me

Ask of Me, and I will give You the nations for Your inheritance, and the ends of the earth for Your possession.

Psalm 2:8

In July 2000 Sue and I sat on the edge of our bed, which almost filled our small bedroom, seeking God's direction. The background hum of the air conditioner reminded me of the oppressive heat outside. I turned the envelope over in my hand. It contained the invitation to *Amsterdam 2000,* a conference for leaders and evangelists hosted by the Billy Graham Association. I had to confirm my air ticket from Singapore to Amsterdam within the next hour.

"I'm a little confused," I confided to Sue. "When this invitation came, I felt a strong conviction that I should attend. I even told our travel agent that we would have no trouble raising the finance for the trip."

"Well," she said, "all we can do right now is go back to the Lord and ask Him what the story is."

I tried not to look at my watch as I stilled my racing thoughts. *Had I been presumptuous in booking this ticket? Was it just a fanciful ego trip to be invited to such a conference?*

"Lord," I prayed, "if you want me to go to Amsterdam for this conference, as we sense you do, please come through for us right now."

The steady whir of the air conditioner continued as we waited quietly for the Lord to give us understanding. While I was prepared to call the travel agent and cancel the ticket, I still felt an inexplicable rising of faith.

Just then the telephone rang. I leaned over to answer it.

"Hello, David. It's Eva here." A retired Chinese-Singaporean schoolteacher in her seventies, Eva was one of my favorites. Forthright in her love for people, she had already led fifty-six Singaporeans into a personal relationship with Christ that year. The previous Sunday, Sue, knowing of Eva's great love for evangelism, had given her a brochure about the conference. She had not mentioned my lack of funds for the trip.

Eva's staccato, Singaporean-clipped voice punched out her message. "David, you must go to that conference. It's urgent. I have talked to some friends, and we have raised the money for your air ticket."

"How did you know I needed finance?" I asked, hardly able to believe this phone call.

"The Lord prompted me," she said.

Of course! How else could she have known? This was certainly a dramatic answer to our prayer.

I looked at my watch. Still half an hour before the deadline with the travel agent.

"Eva," I said, "Thank you for obeying the Lord. Your gift is a huge relief."

"I wish all our prayers were answered that quickly," said Sue, laughing. "You'd better pack!"

I had no idea as the airplane touched down in the thriving city of Amsterdam, only two days after Eva's phone call, that my small, seemingly insignificant step was the first in a new dimension of my faith walk.

My spirit stirred as ten thousand evangelists and leaders gathered from around the world in the bustling mega city. Seated in the huge auditorium, I was challenged to extend my thinking and approach to world evangelism. Day after day, I enjoyed meeting people from around the globe, heard inspirational messages, and went to workshops on every imaginable type of evangelism. The conference had almost finished, and while it was all first class, so far I had seen no momentous reason for my being there, especially in the light of the dramatic last-minute provision of finance to. Had I missed something?

I left the large conference center with a tall, lanky American, Mark Anderson, the director of Impact World Tour (IWT). I knew of Mark through our mutual involvement on the YWAM leadership team. I respected his courage and focus in using modern ways of communicating the unchanging gospel of Jesus Christ, especially to youth. As I walked briskly alongside him, keeping the pace his long strides marked out, our conversation soon turned to our area of mutual interest—evangelism. "How's Impact World Tour going?" I asked as we walked along the small narrow streets, often catching a whiff of the sharp, pungent smell of cannabis wafting out of some hotel.

"Great!" Mark said, and he began to outline the effect of large-scale campaigns in some cities around the world. As he talked, I remembered vividly our last leadership meeting in Fortaleza, situated on the northern coast of Brazil, in 1998. Fortaleza had a reputation for violent gangs and a high incidence of child sex trafficking. For three of those evenings we joined stadium crowds in hot, humid conditions for IWT presentations. For two hours before the evening meetings, I saw traffic backed up outside the stadium. The master of ceremonies pleaded with the Christians present to stay away from the stadium meetings the next two nights so that those who needed to hear the gospel would have room to get in. I was deeply impressed by the contemporary, innovative presentations and testimonies given by the three evangelistic teams. First, Team Xtreme International, a group of superstrong athletes, bent steel, broke concrete blocks, and performed great exploits of strength. On the following night, Island Breeze presented the gospel through Polynesian dance. On the final night, GX International, a team of young hiphop dancers, bike riders, roller bladers, and skate boarders dazzled the Brazilian crowd. Members from each team told of the power of Christ to transform their lives. Over thirty-six thousand people responded to Christ at campaign events, and approximately one hundred thousand came to Christ that year in Fortaleza during other related evangelistic activities following the IWT campaigns.

"It's incredible, Dave. In India recently, up to ten thousand people per day indicated their acceptance of Christ during the IWT campaigns. We've come a long way since our humble beginnings in 1993," he said with a wry smile.

Nearing the YWAM Training Center in de Poort, where we were both staying, I felt a real interest in Mark and the vision he carried for impacting cities, especially as my role at the time included that of Urban Missions Director. *Perhaps we could work together with Mark in Asian cities?*

"Let's talk some more," I said.

"Sure. Let's get something to eat first," Mark replied.

Together with two New Zealanders who were also working with the tour, we made our way to a quiet outside table overlooking the canal at the restaurant opposite the center.

Mark related how he had begun IWT in Wisconsin, USA, attempting to use elements of youth culture to communicate the gospel message.

Going Deeper
The Beginnings of Impact World Tour

I had been working with an evangelistic organization and noticed that almost all the people attending the campaigns had gray hair. I began to experiment with ways I thought would appeal to young people. Music, visual arts, dance, and personal real-life stories were all important elements of youth culture.

I began in 1993 in Wisconsin with nothing. Sometimes I would travel thousands of miles in a week to share the vision and raise finances for IWT. I had only a concept to share with pastors, business, and community leaders. I had no stories to tell, no staff, no finance, not even teams! Eventually I recruited a couple of skaters who knew the Lord. I asked Kevin Stark from Sports Excellence to perform some feats of strength, and we invited Island Breeze to perform. I had to train counselors, preach, operate the sound and lights, run cables, and oversee the video production. Wonderfully, three thousand people showed up at the first evening. Hundreds of kids were there with their skateboards. Some ushers rushed to find me, reporting that some young people had drugs with them outside the venue.

"Don't worry—they're the ones we are reaching," I said. When I gave the altar call, approximately five hundred people responded. Some young people voluntarily surrendered the drugs they had on them.

God had put in our hands a culturally relevant tool for effective proclamation of the gospel in public places that had potential to see hundreds of thousands come to Christ. We took as our motto for IWT, "The Gospel for every person, every nation, every generation."

Mark Anderson
Founder and International Director, Impact World Tour

"So," I said, "it seems that IWT is a tool, like a hammer that has potential to break open cities for the gospel. Perhaps we could work together in some cities in Asia."

"I'd love to do that too, Dave," Mark replied, again with a wry smile. "It makes sense to me. Right now, however, I am focused on your country, New Zealand, with IWT."

"New Zealand?" I asked. "Why New Zealand?"

Mark leaned toward me over the table, still holding his untouched drink. I sensed his intensity.

"In 1995 the YWAM Pacific leaders asked me to bring a fundraising presentation to their meeting in Auckland, New Zealand. After three days in a small meeting room I still had not brought my presentation. During one very ordinary meeting, led by a worship leader with a slightly out of tune guitar, I repented of my proud and critical attitude. I suddenly became aware of the presence of God in the room. I began shaking and I saw a vision of a tidal wave fanning out from New Zealand into the whole of the Pacific and Asia region and then to the rest of the world."

Tidal wave! I immediately pictured a tidal wave Sue had described recently of thousands of people coming to faith in Christ as a huge wave broke on the East Coast of New Zealand. My spiritual antenna went into full alert.

Mark put down his drink. "The worship leader put down his guitar and we took turns to pray. When my turn came, I was still shaking. I spoke out the tidal wave vision. Other leaders also sensed a new impetus in New Zealand and the Pacific. We prayed for the next three hours. During the following three days, we sought God for His purposes in the Pacific region, knowing He had interrupted our plans and schedules. I never did bring the fundraising presentation!"

Mark's angular features seemed set in determination.

"I felt an unusual weight of responsibility to see New Zealand reevangelized. My immediate response was to be willing to change all the plans we had for cities in other nations. Over the next five years, I began to visit New Zealand regularly.

"In January 2000, during one of my visits, Loren Cunningham was also in New Zealand, leading a three-month leadership training school. Over lunch one day Loren enthused over the enormous contribution New Zealanders had made to Youth With A Mission.

" 'By the mid-1980s,' he said, 'New Zealand was the largest mission-sending nation per capita in the Western world. Yet, by the onset of the new millennium, there seemed to be great spiritual poverty in the land.'

"I can still hear the rich timbre of Loren's voice," Mark continued, "as he asked me the question that has not left me since that day. 'Mark,' Loren said, 'would you help to reevangelize New Zealand?'

"I was deeply grateful for Loren's outstanding leadership and encouragement in launching Impact World Tour through Youth With a Mission. I knew that by his question he was asking me if I would invest time in New Zealand and bring Impact World Tour to the whole nation, not to just one city."

Leaning forward again, Mark slowed his speech. "Dave," he said, "I yearn to see whole nations impacted with the gospel, not just cities and towns."

I nodded slowly in agreement. "How did you respond to Loren?" I asked.

"I could not give him an answer that day," Mark said. "As I met with him over the next two days, I began to respond at a deep level to meet this mammoth request. I had no idea how we could undertake such a large project with the limited personnel and resources we had at the time. Besides we already had heavy commitments in other nations around the world—India, Brazil, Holland, and Scandinavia."

"Don't you think there would be greater response to campaign evangelism in some of those nations than in New Zealand?" I asked. I had only heard recent reports of spiritual decline from my nation.

Mark looked me up and down. I sensed he carried something in his heart that I had not grasped.

"That was exactly the struggle I faced when Loren first put that question to me. As I wrestled with Loren's proposal, I realized that, like many western nations, New Zealand is a small nation that had once been predominantly Christian. A nationwide sweep proclaiming the gospel could play a part in beginning to turn the country to its Christian roots."

Now, that was a concept that excited me!

"Are you interested in coming down, Dave?" Mark asked. "Ross here is helping pioneer the NZ project."

I shook my head. "It's a great vision you have for New Zealand, Mark, but we are committed to Asia. I'd love to work with you in some Asian cities. The scale of evangelism that you are heading into thrills me. Ross will do a great job, I am sure. If there is any way I can assist, let me know."

Mark said nothing as he stretched his neck. Then glancing at his watch he said, "We'd better get some sleep now. Will you be at the YWAM International Staff conference in New Zealand in September?"

"Yes," I replied. "I guess I'll see you there."

As I lay down that night, I felt that I would see more of Mark in the future. I drifted off to sleep thinking of the night's conversation and the millions in Asia who had never heard of Jesus Christ. Mark's comment repeated in my mind. "I yearn to see whole nations impacted with the gospel." I had no doubt that connecting with Mark was the main purpose for my trip to Amsterdam.

September 2000: New Zealand

Before long I was again seated on board an aircraft headed to Auckland, the largest city in New Zealand. During the past two months I often relived my brief encounter with Mark Anderson in the Amsterdam restaurant. The concept of large-scale evangelism enthralled me. Although we still loved Asia, I had begun to experience a vague stirring in my spirit that I had come to recognize as a heralding of a new venture. I felt that it was time for an Asian leader to take my regional role in South East Asia and that the Lord could be opening new opportunities for us. Repeatedly I was alerted by the familiar inner prompting of the Holy Spirit. *A wide door of effective service is open to you.*

Reaching for my Bible in the pocket on the aircraft seat in front of me, I looked up the familiar Scripture reference and read, "A great and effective door has opened to me, and there are many adversaries" (1 Corinthians 16:9). I read it again. And again. Was God opening a new door for us? Were we to have some involvement in this venture in New Zealand? Was I to have a role in what seemed an impossible task? I hoped that this trip would answer some of my questions.

The 747 descended over the sprawling city, the green volcanoes punctuating the array of single-story houses. The rolling green hills at the edge of the city sang out their welcome. It felt good to be on New Zealand soil again.

This time I joined one thousand of our staff who had gathered from all around the world to attend the YWAM staff conference. Filing into the large auditorium, staff members everywhere greeted one another—young and old, Asian, Hispanic, Islanders, and Caucasian. It was like a family reunion.

I could easily see Mark Anderson's tall frame at the front of the auditorium. I was excited to see him again.

"Hey, Dave!" he said, warmly embracing me. "Let's get together again at lunch."

The meeting came to order and moved through worship, followed by reports from all around the world. How privileged I was to be part of this large, diverse YWAM family!

Mark was more direct this time as we collected our lunch from the long food line. Coming straight to the point, he said in a matter-of-fact voice, "Dave, I want you to pray about returning to New Zealand and leading this nationwide project."

I hardly heard the laughter, the rise and fall of voices, and the clatter of cutlery as other YWAM staff met over lunch. Finding my voice as we sat down in some spare seats in the middle of one of the long tables, I managed to say, "Don't you already have leaders in place?"

"Well," said Mark, "the New Zealander who was going to head up this project was not able to continue, so we really need someone who knows New Zealand and who has strong relationships in the churches to give leadership to this project."

Mark continued. "There is a young surfer, Jay Lucas, who has just returned from working on campaigns in Australia. He is itching to get started. Other church leaders around the nation have also expressed some initial support."

"Mark," I said, "since I met you in Amsterdam, I have often thought about this project in New Zealand. I am excited about it. I hadn't thought of being involved on the ground though."

I looked at the YWAMers around us, chatting over lunch. "I'll have to pray about it with Sue before I can give you an answer."

When I called Sue, who had remained in Singapore, to relate Mark's invitation to return to New Zealand, she was completely taken aback. "We can't uproot the family again," she said. "But I will pray about it."

While I sensed a wonderful opportunity opening in New Zealand, I knew how important it was to be in agreement with my wife on major decisions. I understood it would be difficult for her to capture the dynamic of the staff conference and the importance and urgency of this huge task. To move our family would be like turning a ship going full steam in one direction. However, I knew that Sue would go to the Lord, and I trusted God to direct her personally. I was comforted by the stirrings toward change we both felt over the last few months.

Toward the end of the conference in New Zealand, Mark gave a brief inspiring message, which he referred to as the "All" message. He repeated the mandate Christ gave us to "go into all the world and preach the gospel to every creature." Mark emphasized the importance of taking the whole gospel to the whole world—that meant to every person, people group, nation, and generation. He outlined again the vision from the Lord to impact New Zealand with the gospel on a large scale. I felt an increasing desire to be involved. Again I sensed the familiar prompting of the Holy Spirit. *I have opened a wide door of effective service for you.*

Was the Lord asking us to return to New Zealand? "Lord if this is you, I am willing," I prayed.

When I called Sue again, I was surprised to find her enthusiastic and eager to move. "Dave," she said, "it's the other side of the boat!"

"What do you mean?" I asked.

"I was reading John 21. Peter had been fishing all night and caught nothing. He was tired and discouraged. Jesus told him to cast the net on the other side of the boat. When he obeyed that command from the Lord, there were so many fish that he was not able to draw the net in. I feel just like Peter must have—tired and weary, with little to show for many hours of work. Perhaps Impact World Tour is a different strategy for evangelism that the Lord is inviting us to be part of. There may be a great harvest in New Zealand. This could be the 'combine harvester' we have often dreamed of."

As we talked more, we both sensed the Lord was directing us to take up this challenge.

When I saw Mark the following day, I shared with him our willingness to return to New Zealand. His face relaxed in a broad grin. "That's great news, Dave!" he said. "We've been praying for New Zealand for the past six years. I really believe you are the person to lead this project."

Immediately we began to seek the Lord about the unique strategy for the tour. I soon discovered in Mark a remarkable ability to think and plan strategically and to work out in practical ways the vision to see the gospel preached throughout a nation. His experience in conducting campaigns was invaluable in laying a foundation for understanding the spiritual and practical components that would be necessary in this nationwide undertaking. At the same time, I recognized the importance of strong relational networks and an understanding of New Zealand culture and protocol for a successful venture.

"Mark," I said, "if this is going to work in New Zealand, there is one good friend and fellow leader you must meet, Trevor Yaxley, director of Lifeway Ministries."

"Right, let's go then." Mark was never one to delay when it was time to take action.

Trevor greeted us enthusiastically as he walked toward us in the Lifeway office, still limping, I noted, from a car accident ten years earlier. I regarded Trevor as an outstanding, courageous, apostolic leader in New Zealand, passionate about evangelizing New Zealand. Sue and I had enjoyed working with him in the early 1990s during the Rise Up Campaign, a nationwide thrust to unify and mobilize the Church of New Zealand in evangelism. Bold, fervent prayer and aggressive evangelism were features during the training time. As teams moved around the nation, working with over seven hundred participating churches, over five thousand people committed their lives to Jesus Christ, and approximately the same number rededicated their lives to the Lord.

Unsurprisingly, when we shared the vision of IWT with Trevor, he responded positively. After praying with his leadership team, he agreed to partner with us.

"Dave," he said, "I've always wanted to work with you since the Rise Up Campaigns."

"It's a great comfort to have your involvement, Trev," I said. "I have a hunch that we will need the zeal and drive of the Lifeway crew to see this project come about. We will also need a whole army of believers across the nation."

As we made the return journey to Auckland, I asked Mark a question that I had been mulling over during the last twenty-four hours. "Mark, what do you think the greatest challenge will be for us in New Zealand?"

Without hesitating, Mark answered, "Faith. You're going to have to persevere in faith, Dave. In the meetings I have been involved with so far, people have been very positive to IWT but also very cautious. I literally 'lent' my faith to some as they considered hosting such an endeavor in their town. You may have to do the same."

Mark and I spent more time together over the next days, planning, strategizing, and discussing details of what it would mean to conduct a nationwide tour. I began to realize the enormity of the task and just how much faith I would need.

My faith had already begun to rise in response to the specific words the Lord had spoken to Sue and me. I could hardly wait to return to New Zealand through this "open door" and to begin this new adventure.

Chapter Three

Small Beginnings

Auckland, January 2001

The next three months passed in a whirl of activity—saying farewell to our many friends in Singapore, packing, planning, and preparing. Our younger children relished the idea of a new adventure in their home country, which they had seen very little of since moving overseas. Perhaps the move was hardest for our teenage daughter, Lisa, as all her friends were in Singapore. I felt it could be emotionally difficult for her to uproot.

We quickly set up home near the YWAM Training Centre in South Auckland. Our three younger children took little time adjusting to the more relaxed New Zealand culture, going about barefoot and enjoying sports and a more outdoor lifestyle. Their Singaporean accents soon faded, although their love for Asian food did not!

Jay Lucas, a part-Maori YWAMer in his late twenties, greeted us enthusiastically.

"Hey, man," he said, embracing me in a bear hug, "I couldn't believe it when I heard you guys were coming back. We were dancing around the office! Let's get this show on the road!"

I liked Jay. For the past few years he had been working with IWT in Australia. When I last saw Jay, he was spending every spare moment in the surf, so I admired the way he was willing to stay out of the water and spend long hours working on the tour logistics.

"You know, Dave," he said, pulling his shoulder-length hair back into a pony tail, "when I saw hundreds of people rush forward at altar calls in Tasmania and Queensland, it was more than worthwhile. It's going to be awesome in New Zealand." My own wholehearted enthusiasm was tempered by the reality of the challenges that lay ahead. As I surveyed Jay's office, which consisted of a mobile phone, laptop computer, and a surfboard, I realized just how far we had to go to establish a nationwide campaign.

One of the first steps was to train city facilitators for the campaign, and with this in mind we conducted our first three-month training school. I greeted our school leader, Jenny Mollison, at the airport. Jenny was an Australian woman in her thirties who came up only to my shoulder. Mark had assured me that Jenny was already a veteran in training coordinators and overseeing many aspects of the tour. "It's great to have you here, Jenny." I liked her open, unassuming face. "Some of the students are already arriving."

Jenny may have been short in stature, but she soon showed her huge capacity for behind-the-scenes work preparing for the training school and tour. Since she had led several training schools, Jenny was very familiar with all that was involved, so I was surprised when she was having difficulty planning the essential first week of the school. "I don't get it, Dave," she lamented, half-laughing. "I have prayed and asked the Lord, but I don't have any clarity for the first week. Maybe God has something up His sleeve that we can't see yet."

When we heard that George Otis Jr. was speaking at a Transformation Seminar in Auckland during the dates of that first week, we had no doubt that this was God's plan for the training school for the first week.

The students came from all over the world and from different cultures. Among them were Caucasian and Maori New Zealanders, Asians, Americans, Pacific Islanders, and Europeans. The oldest student was 73. What a diverse group, I thought.

As we listened to George Otis's teaching from his documentation of over two hundred communities in the developing world that had undergone radical transformation, faith began to grow in our hearts that towns and cities in New Zealand could be transformed into godly, thriving, loving communities.

Transformation, according to George Otis Jr., is:

> A neighborhood or city whose values and institutions are overrun by God. Divine fire has not only been summoned, it has fallen. It is a culture that has been impacted by the full measure of the Kingdom of God. A society in which supernatural power flows like a river of molten lava, altering everything and everyone in its path.[1]

We began to see IWT as a small part in God's overall plan for the nation. We realized that campaign evangelism was to be a catalyst to trigger the harvest in New Zealand and ultimately help bring about transformation. Although 54 percent of the population of New Zealand claimed to be Christian,[2] we realized that as a nation we were a long way from the picture of transformed society George Otis Jr. painted. Transformation was a long-term, multifaceted process, far beyond our immediate scope. It would require hard work, faith, prayer, love, and cooperation of many people working in every sphere of society, including business, politics, education, science and technology, media, and arts and entertainment. Our immediate response was simply to carry out the task God had put in our hand.

Returning to New Zealand was a great shock to our family in many ways. Before long we realized how far moral values among New Zealand young people had fallen. In a way we were introduced to its stark reality through a friend of our teenage daughter. Her short life brought home to us the cry of this generation and its need to know the love of God in a personal way.

I grew increasingly concerned for our fifteen-year-old daughter, Lisa, who was spending more time in her room and on the Internet. *More than normal,* I thought. It was the gradual change in her mood and behavior, however, that caused me to find out what was going on. Her normal bubbly personality had become withdrawn, her laughing blue eyes clouded.

"What's up, Lisa?" I asked gently, sensing she could easily rebuff my effort to draw her out. Lisa shrugged and turned away. As I sat next to her on her bed, my hand on her shoulder, I could only hear the loud ticking of the clock.

"We've been concerned..." I began.

"It's Amy," Lisa interrupted. Tears started to roll down Lisa's cheeks as the pain she carried for her friend, Amy, came pouring out. I thought of Amy. Her cropped black hair framed a too thin face. Behind her glasses, her eyes were wistful, doleful, but I found it hard to believe she was suicidal.

"Are you sure, Lisa?"

"Dad, she's already tried to cut her wrists. Look," she said.

I knew that Lisa would not breach loyalty to a close friend by showing me e-mails she had been receiving unless the situation was desperate, so I appreciated her confidence. As I quickly scanned some of Amy's e-mails written over the last six months, a clear picture came to mind of a girl searching for love. Amy had grown up in a home where her father was often absent because of his work commitments. As Amy struggled with the death of one of her friends, she had doubts about God's love for her. She was left wondering whom she could trust or whether anyone could really show her God's love. She started finding comfort for the ache in her heart through unhealthy eating patterns and drinking alcohol, which she managed to hide from her mother for a time. She could not, however, hide the growing depression that closed in on her, eventually pulling her into a seemingly unreachable abyss. "Lately," Amy had written, "the only prayer I pray is that I die. Quickly."

I prayed with Lisa and then contacted some experienced counselors who lived near Amy to see if they could help her. We continued to pray for her. Lisa, with increasing concern and anxiety, was daily communicating with her through MSN.

Other young people we knew of were also in difficult situations:

Joy's Story

Joy was home with her sister for the weekend. As the family settled down to enjoy the news, Joy's father was surprised as his older daughter determinedly walked to the TV and turned it off. "Joy has something to tell you, Dad," she said grimly. Taking her cue from her older sister, Joy managed to break the news of her pregnancy, punctuated by sobs. "I'm so sorry," she finished, looking at the floor. Gone was her defiant "I can do what I want" attitude of her earlier teenage years; she now expressed the humility of adult responsibility.

Although visibly stunned, Joy's parents managed to find comfort and assurance for their much loved seventeen-year-old daughter and embraced her. All three cried together. "We'll stand by you, Joy," they said, "and help you find your own way through this." Seven months later they doted on their firstborn grandson and continued to support their daughter.

Joy and her son were fortunate. 16,410 babies conceived in similar situations in 2001 were aborted in New Zealand.

Anthony's Story

You could not find a young person with more potential. Anthony was athletic, well built, a high achiever in school, and had a delightful sense of humor. Somehow during his teenage years he found it easy to be "one of the boys." By the time he was sixteen, he was regularly binge drinking. His grades slipped, his humor faded, and he spent many solitary hours in his bedroom. Life turned gray for Anthony. He left school, lived for the weekends when he could drink into oblivion, and eventually was drinking too much most nights. Before long, drugs provided a comfort that alcohol could not. After four years of alcohol and drug abuse, Anthony eventually acknowledged his problem and started the long process of recovery, with help from Alcoholics Anonymous, a supportive family, and two young Christian friends who remained committed in friendship to him, even on his worst days, when he reverted to old habits.

Anthony was one of 125,000 binge-drinking teens in New Zealand.[3]

What I found remarkable was that Amy, Joy, and Anthony all came from Christian homes. As preteens they had all been strong believers. What had happened to them—and to this generation of young people, known as GenX—to cause them to become cynical toward Christian values?

One friend and long-term missionary gave helpful insight into how this generation had come to such a state. "You see, Dave," he said, "these kids are where they are because of the 'gospel' they have been listening to."

"Gospel!" I thought. "Most kids don't even know the gospel."

"Think about what this generation is exposed to," he continued. "The theory of evolution, thousands of messages on violence, and exposure to as many if not more sexually seductive messages or explicit sex on TV, sex education taught in schools without any moral commitment, and the passing of recent laws in our government that encourage a changing morality."

I thought with shame at the arrogance of my generation, the baby boomer generation. We had largely rejected moral values, divorced our spouses, defied authority, and marched in moratoriums. We were blinded to our pride toward the previous generation.

Generation Xers were largely the children of abandonment, of wounded relationships, of broken promises. They were familiar with disappointment and with the marriage breakup of their parents. They struggled to find people they could trust and, when they did, drew answers from their peers to make sense of a world vastly different from the world previous generations had known. Whereas our generation had known high ideals, in their world of blurred morals, truth was largely measured by their own experience. Now our youth, including Amy, Joy, and Anthony, faced major social problems with binge drinking, depression, crime, and a high degree of sexual activity with little responsibility.

Left to ourselves, we had drifted. Cardinal Thomas S. Williams, the Catholic leader of New Zealand, said, "Our failure to protect basic values and rudimentary citizenship is fast converting our country into a moral wasteland." He went on to bemoan the undermining of the value of the traditional family unit as essential to the well-being of society.[4]

New Zealand is still a young nation. One New Zealand historian feels that within the last century "the conflicts of human history have been played out more intensively and more rapidly in New Zealand than anywhere else on Earth."[5] Resident in its breathtaking beauty is fantastic, rough, glorious, and dangerous places. Inherent in the destiny of this nation is a rare quality that has the potential to bring hope to the world. Sean Astin, who played Sam Gamgee in the *Lord of the Rings* trilogy, summed this up at the premier of *The Return of the King* in Wellington: "It's such a tenuous time on the planet. So much darkness and so much villainy in the world, but this city and this county are a beacon of hope. Your warm, bright smiling faces, your huge hearts and your enormous welcoming spirit are a hope for the world."[6]

Our failure to protect basic values and rudimentary citizenship is fast converting our country into a moral wasteland.

Lisa's friend Amy was one who did not receive that hope. She sank further into an abyss of depression from which she could find no way out. We were unprepared for the finality of her suicide. Lisa was consumed by grief—this fierce, brutal intruder shaking her world. Exposed and alone, she could find no answer to the haunting questions of "Why?" and "What if?" We had prayed often for Amy and trusted God to heal her life. I had no keys to empower Lisa. I had no simple answers that could answer the depth of the cry of her heart as she wrestled with complex issues. Her countenance clouded as she questioned her own faith in God and struggled with the heartache of losing Amy.

I thought of the thousands of Amys in New Zealand. They might not all choose the same final outcome as Amy, but they all needed to know love and acceptance in a real way. Those who struggle with the same issues she did, of finding love, of being allowed to question without being pressured to conform.

Going Deeper

Some New Zealand Statistics: 2001

Births to unmarried parents:
44 percent of all children born

Children in sole parent families:
31 percent of children younger than 15

Number of abortions:
16,410

Youth suicide rate:
20 per 100,000 population

Recorded violent offences:
100 per 10,000 population

Source: New Zealand Census 2001

Somehow our struggle with Lisa through the pain Amy had battled and eventually lost to gave identity and personality to the pain of this generation. It was not just New Zealand youth with the highest suicide rate in the developed world, so many abused, so many fatherless, so many teenage pregnancies. Amy put a face on this restless sea of youthful humanity that needed to know Jesus. We may have lost the battle for Amy, but I renewed my resolve to involve as many as possible in reaching as many of our youth as possible with the message of the beauty and love of Jesus through Impact World Tour.

Chapter Four

Open the Gates

Lift up your heads, O you gates!
And be lifted up, you everlasting doors!
And the King of glory shall come in.

Psalm 24:7

As our first IWT Training School students and staff gathered daily, we filled the small classroom with prayer. It soon became our highest priority. We established a "fasting" roster, where at least two staff or students set aside some time each day to withdraw from food and to pray for New Zealand and the coming campaign. Although we had much to learn in the dynamics of campaign infrastructure, I insisted that we begin each day with prayer for the nation. The task of reevangelizing a nation seemed almost unattainable, considering our available resources. God would have to step in and multiply our small efforts. Some mornings we abandoned our teaching curriculum and continued in prayer. Sometimes we did not feel like praying, but believing that anything accomplished through IWT was first accomplished through prayer, we pushed on. Sometimes our prayers seemed feeble before our mighty God, dry and shallow, the weakness of our own flesh binding them to the earth. At other times, we boldly declared God's promises to our nation and to one another. No matter how we felt, we persevered in prayer.

We were often impressed to pray for the Maori of New Zealand, the indigenous or host people of the land. As the school progressed, our prayers intensified and our desire to work with the Maori increased.

Honor the gatekeepers, Dave. I felt the Lord was giving us a key to unlock the involvement of the Maori people.

After a particularly intense time of prayer, I felt we needed to turn our prayer to action. "These last few weeks," I said, as we concluded our prayer time, "as we have been praying for the Maori, I have felt we need to invite their input into this nationwide project. We need to honor their standing as important gatekeepers in the land."

Seeing the blank expressions of those who were not New Zealanders, I tried to explain this concept. "Because the Maori were the first inhabitants of New Zealand, God gave them a crucial authority or guardianship. This is still relevant in today's world. I have felt a growing conviction over these weeks that we should visit the Maori people in each city where we plan to bring IWT. We need to go in a spirit of honor and humility and ask their blessing and participation in Impact World Tour."

I opened the Scriptures that had become so familiar to me over these beginning weeks of the school and read, "Lift up your heads, O you gates! And be lifted up, you everlasting doors! And the King of glory shall come in" (Psalm 24:7).

"As we have been asking God for His strategy for IWT, we feel that we are to go through the 'gates' in the land by honoring the gatekeepers. The indigenous gate is not the only gate we need to acknowledge. We will also need to go through the church and, where appropriate, the civic gates.

"Let's pray together and seek God's wisdom," I said.

Jay Lucas, being part-Maori, was first to respond. "We've got to do this!" he said, his excited voice rising. "We've got to go to the first people of the land!"

Eileen Williams, our seventy-three-year-old student, was amazed that the love she had been carrying for the Maori for many years could begin to be expressed.

Jenny Mollison said, "I had a hunch this tour was going to be different from any tour I have been on. We need to respond to the Lord's specific direction for us."

All our staff and students agreed that visiting the Maori people was the next step for us.

I approached Monte Ohia, a Maori leader associated with the YWAM Auckland Training Centre, to join us for the proposed Maori Gates Tour, as we called the forthcoming tour. As a respected leader amongst his people who had been an advisor in Maori and Pacific education and affairs, I felt he could assist us in many aspects of Maori culture. He confirmed what the Lord was saying to us.

Going Deeper

Why the Indigenous Gate?

The world is a series of inheritances and jurisdictions under God. New Zealand's place in Polynesia is no accident. The *Tangata Whenua* (host people of the land) carry a unique responsibility as spiritual gatekeepers. Maori leaders, such as the late Norman Tawhiao, have demonstrated the importance of cleansing and healing the foundations of the land before building in the new generation. Confession, repentance, and reconciliation have become the themes of the national prayer movement, particularly since 1990, and Maori leadership has come to the front in many parts of national life, including the Church. I believe this is right and pleasing to God.

It was seen as appropriate, therefore, to do something unprecedented: to take the time to travel through New Zealand seeking the blessing of the guardians of each indigenous inheritance. We called this the Maori Gates Tour.

John Dawson
Founder and Director of International Reconciliation Coalition
President, Youth With A Mission

With Monte advising us in various aspects of Maori protocol, we spent time over the next months praying and consulting with Maori eldership and other preparations for the approaching Maori Gates Tour.

Our core team of fifteen Impact World Tour members, together with Monte and Linda Ohia, met in the YWAM training school courtyard on January 21, 2002, to seek God's blessing as we departed on our historic Maori Gates Tour. I stressed to the team that this tour was to honor the Maori people and their place in the land. It was not a political tactic or patronizing act to gain favor. It was a strategy borne out of the heart of God. I believed it could trigger a great harvest in the coming days, not only in young Maori, but also among other ethnic and cultural groups in the land.

"These weeks of visiting *marae* around New Zealand are about honor. We will trust God to open the hearts of the people, and thus the gates. If the local people do not want IWT to come to their area, we will respect that."

Monte added a brief explanation of Maori protocol. "Remember," he said, "we are guests on each *marae* we will visit. We must honor each tribal group and their protocol. That is the only way to go."

After our first visit to a *marae*, the meeting place of a local tribe, in the northern city of Whangarei, we headed south to Huntly, an hour's drive from Auckland. Our core group swelled to almost one hundred as friends and interested people gathered with us at the entrance way to the Maori queen's marae, Waahi Marae, near Huntly. I was glad that John Dawson, the founder of the International Reconciliation Coalition, was able to accompany us for this part of the tour. The afternoon sun highlighted the shades of green displayed in the surrounding bush-covered rolling hills. The Waikato River flowed steadily nearby the marae. A hush came over our group. Monte Ohia, as the senior Maori elder in our group, reassured our guests, "If you've not been to a *powhiri*, or Maori welcome, just follow us. Try and catch in your spirit what God is doing here. We can explain later."

As the welcome cry rang out, we slowly walked forward into the large grassy area in front of the meeting house. One of the tribal warriors, in full Maori dress, lunged forward, wielding his spear in both offensive and defensive stances. John Dawson, as the recognized senior spiritual leader in our group, stooped to pick up the challenge the Maori warrior placed in front of us. I thought of the real challenge that lay ahead in preparation for IWT. Yes, we were coming in peace, but we knew that we would also encounter battles ahead in establishing the vision in the land.

The marae elders welcomed us both in the Maori and in English. Monte Ohia, John Dawson, and I alternated our greetings, which were interspersed with songs.

Monte, speaking in Maori, affirmed the presence of *Io,* the Maori name for Creator God, and his Son Jesus Christ. He honored the Maori and their place in the land. Quoting Acts 17:26-27 he also affirmed the equality of all races under God. *"And He has made from one blood every nation of men to dwell on all the face of the earth, and has determined their preappointed times and the boundaries of their dwellings, so that they should seek the Lord, in the hope that they might grope for Him and find Him, though He is not far from each one of us."*

John Dawson referred briefly to his personal journey of reconciliation with, deep love for, and acceptance by the Maori. "Over the centuries, God's footprints can be seen in both our cultures as we have walked our pathways. Just as God deals with us as individuals to bring us into friendship and sonship with Himself, so He deals with nations and cultures. We can be resistant, blinded, and ignorant to the wooing of God's Spirit, as He demonstrates His love toward us. We love our sin yet have a deep yearning for righteousness. In our personal history, there are flickers of light and hope interspersed with moments of great shame. So it is as God deals with any culture."

John eloquently continued to call forth a destiny in New Zealand of all peoples living in harmony.

When it was my turn to speak, I stepped forward. I did not have words to express all that was in my heart at that time. I was sobered by the host of New Zealand Christians who had gone before us and the immensity of the task ahead of us. I believed this was a unique time in the history of New Zealand. I believed we would eventually see again God's righteousness in every area of society. I believed we would see many people come to faith in Christ through Impact World Tour. "Thank you for your welcome," I concluded.

After the final song, the local people welcomed us with the traditional Maori *hongi*. As we pressed noses with each of our brothers and sisters, we felt warmly and officially welcomed.

Going Deeper
What Is a Powhiri?

Powhiri is the Maori word for welcome ceremony. Resident within the Maori culture, as in every culture, are redemptive gifts that well represent the yearning of the heart of God for fellowship and unity among His people. The *marae,* which is the meeting place of the local tribal group, is a virtual village reflecting community, fellowship, and extended family.

When the visitors are welcomed onto the marae, a tribal warrior advances toward them wielding a spear in offensive and defensive stances. A challenge by the warrior is an invitation to test the intent of the visitors and their motivation for coming. The warrior places a token, usually in the form of a twig or leaf, on the ground. If the visitors pick it up, they are coming in peace.

A local Maori woman issues a call of welcome to the visitors as is appropriate as they enter the meeting house. In response to the welcome, another woman entering with the visitors cries out, "*Karanga mai, Karanga mai, Karanga mai!*" (Call us again, call us again, call us again!)

Once the visitors are at the front and facing the local host people, *Kaumatua* (tribal elder) give a traditional speech of welcome in the Maori tongue. This is followed by a song. A leader representing the visiting group responds, and they in turn present their song. This process is usually repeated at least three times.

Following the speeches, the host people and visitors come together and *hongi.* This is a greeting in which noses are pressed together. This represents the sharing of the breath of God and the life He gives, including its joys and sorrows. The host people and visitors have now become one, and after fellowship and food the general meeting can proceed.

After sharing the generous meal the local people put on for us, we assembled again, this time inside a large hall.

Here we outlined the vision of IWT for the land. I summarized the elements of each performing team that would appeal to Maori: "Young males love the staunch Team Xtreme strong men. Youth respond well to the skate and dance culture of the GX team. Maori families will enjoy the Polynesian and Maori dances of Island Breeze. All team members are committed Christians.

"We want to bring the gospel message of hope, restoration, and reconciliation to the people of New Zealand through the power and love of Jesus Christ."

Monte brought our presentation to a close. He reaffirmed the importance of the Maori Gate and appealed to the elders to open the gate to us.

We quietly sat and waited while the elders conferred amongst themselves. I hardly moved. *What if they think this is just some token act? Or a Western form being imposed upon them.* I prayed silently.

I looked up as a gray-haired elder shuffled forward. He cleared his throat. "Thank you," he said in Maori. "Thank you for coming to our part of the land. If you can bring hope to our people, then you are welcome. We open the gate to you and will support you however we can."

I felt greatly relieved and sensed God's approval toward this small step of faith we had taken.

Later that evening after combined worship in the meeting house, the Maori queen, breaking the normal protocol of having another speak on her behalf, stood. "What tribe can refuse this?" she asked. "I would have teams like this on every marae in the nation." A murmur of approval came from those seated around her. I was touched by the sincerity of her response.

It was not always a simple matter of presenting our vision and asking the Maori to bless it. In one marae the elders seemed initially suspicious of our motives. "You *Pakehas* (white people) would go ahead anyway," one said.

I tried to explain that the whole purpose of our visit was to respect and honor their wishes in regard to IWT.

Others were concerned about their young people forgetting their Maori roots. Jay Lucas and other young Maori in our team helped to break down this barrier.

Jay spoke deliberately but with enthusiasm, "My journey in IWT has helped me realize that I can be both Maori and Christian. We all know people who have adopted a Western form of Christianity or remained so steeped in Maoridom that Christianity has not impacted their lives. Both stands are like a one-wing bird."

On the East Coast, in the city of Gisborne, the first city in the world to see the sun every day, the tall, fine-looking Chinese mayor of Gisborne also welcomed us enthusiastically—in fluent Maori! As we sat together enjoying afternoon tea after the powhiri, he asked me, "Why don't the churches work together more? Doesn't your Book say that you are all one?"

I felt grieved that he, like so many other New Zealanders, regarded the church as a disunited, dysfunctional body.

"For Impact World Tour to be successful in any community, the churches will have to work together," I replied. "You are right. We need to operate more as one."

Christchurch in the South Island had a predominantly English feel, while further south, Dunedin had a strong Scottish heritage. This, coupled with the smaller Maori population in the South Island, would have made it easy to overlook the Maori there. However, we felt we were to obey the Lord and visit marae in the South Island.

In one small marae, as the senior elder stood and opened the gates to the tour in the South Island, his niece challenged him. "Uncle, you have opened the gate to IWT, would you open the door of your heart to Jesus?"

Still standing, with his head slightly bowed, this elder was quiet for a moment, then answered. "Yes. I need to do that. Yes, I open my heart to Jesus, the Savior."

His niece stood alongside him and led him in a prayer of repentance, acknowledging Jesus as the Lord of his life.

"Lord," I prayed, "do the same for many Maori through the tour."

In the marae we visited over the next two weeks, the Maori queen's response was echoed in every place. "If Impact World Tour is a vehicle by which hope and restoration can come to our people, it is welcome."

As our small entourage traveled the two-day return trip from Invercargill, the world's most southern city, we had ample time to reflect and pray. I drove our van-load of staff through the farmland of the deep south, northwards along the east coast. Behind the sheep-dotted hills on our left rose the snow-tipped Southern Alps, forming a backbone through the South Island. The sea stretched endlessly on our right. "How far you have brought me, Lord," I prayed sincerely, "from my early surfing days."

Surrounded by such beauty, I thought of how little of God's blessing we had appropriated as a nation. Monte, seated beside me, echoed my thoughts. "You know, Dave," he mused, "we have a long way to go. Our nation has opened itself to negative forces through unrighteous decisions at a leadership level. There is a huge gap between God's intended blessing and our outworking of that."

"I agree, Monte," I said. "It's righteousness that brings blessing. I've been impressed with the number of people on each marae we have visited so far who genuinely want godliness and right living among their people."

Monte continued, "In the marae we saw how hope rises in young and old alike as they intuitively recognize the need to live in right relationship with God, through Jesus Christ. They don't want religion or man-made rules. They want a demonstration of godliness that works in their communities."

"That's what we all want," I said

When we returned to Auckland, I told the team that in twenty years of ministry I had never experienced so much of God's manifest presence. Our overseas staff had a far greater appreciation for the beauty of the land and its people. One New Zealand businessman, who joined us for part of the tour, had never before been officially welcomed onto a marae, although he had grown up in close geographical proximity. The Maori Gates Tour began in him a journey of a closer alignment with the Maori people.

Jenny said, "We've never done anything like this in IWT before. This brings a different dimension to the campaigns."

John Dawson later concisely summed up the significance of the Maori Gates Tour. "This protocol of humility is a new way to implement a campaign using the values we have taught in the International Reconciliation Coalition. The native people opened their doors, literally and spiritually. Watch for a big harvest beginning January 2004."

Komiti Maori

In March 2003 *Komiti Maori* was formed for the purpose of maximizing the potential for Maori to accept Christ in a life-giving way. This Komiti continued to meet monthly to contribute a Maori perspective to the IWT campaign. With the increase of many ethnic groups in New Zealand, whose expressions also need to be encouraged within the church, I was often asked why we emphasized the *Tangata Whenua* in particular. Komiti Maori issued a foundational document outlining this point.

Going Deeper

These ethnic groups flourish and, in effect, dwell as "children" in New Zealand. They enter into the spiritual, social, and political environment that Maori and Pakeha, as "parents," have established. By principle, as both parents become firmly established in their identities in Christ, they will influence the children in like manner. The parents of this nation, Maori and Pakeha, have a long history together—a journey which was signified by the signing of the covenant agreement, known as the Treaty of Waitangi. The historical entrance into this agreement, by way of treaty covenant, created a partnership, much like marriage, under which all other children who enter this land abide. As we address specific needs for Maori, we in turn engage in a process that encourages us to respond to the needs and concerns of all peoples from varying ethnicities, who make New Zealand their home.

Komiti Maori

New Look for Island Breeze

Meanwhile I encouraged Ray and Shaneane Totorewa, leaders of Island Breeze in New Zealand, to pursue their dream to include a strong Maori expression in the Island Breeze performance. Gathering a small team, they wholeheartedly set to work to create a new presentation that would be specific and relevant for the NZ tour. "It's a huge challenge, Dave," Ray confided, "to effectively communicate the gospel to Maori by Maori. A well-known Maori proverb says, 'We walk into the future backwards,' and while that is good, it can also hold us back from moving forward, unless there is full resolution of some past issues."

I knew that some offenses having to do with the division and devastation left by breaches in the Treaty of Waitangi and some insensitive missionary attempts had left a "bad smell" in the heart of many Maori toward ongoing missionary attempts. I could only advise Ray and Shaneane to act in humility and to present the truth of Jesus Christ in the way that the Lord showed them. "God is leading you. You must respond to Him in faith and obedience and leave the results with Him." So it was for all of us as we continued to lay the foundations for IWT in the land.

Chapter Five

Get on Board!

"I want to say to you dear fellow Kiwis and beloved Christians tonight, get on board this boat of divine purpose. It is of historical importance."

Joy Dawson

August 2001

The day was overcast as I pulled up in front of the drab, gray, four-story building in the center of an industrial South Auckland area. "This is it," I said to Jay and Jenny, who had accompanied me to inspect our office and classroom for the next three years. A businessman had donated the use of the top two floors. We had outgrown our classroom and office and now with this provision needed to expand our operations.

I chose to ignore the buildup of dirt on the unused stairway. Fumbling with the keys, I opened the door to the third-floor office. We were all silent as we surveyed the empty spacious area. A strong musty smell filled the air.

"This is huge!" said Jay. "And we've got the same area on the fourth floor also!"

"Nothing that some cleaning and painting won't fix," Jenny said as we walked toward a large room at the rear of the office. "This would be a great room to meet and strategize in."

"Sounds like a war room on the battlefield. This facility has great potential," I said. Then, surveying the sprawling city extending to the harbor, I added, "Look at the view of Auckland!"

Before long our staff and students set to work cleaning and painting. The new blue coat of paint on the outside of the building lifted the appearance. The installment of donated equipment, tables, desks, wall dividers, telephones, and computers soon transformed our office.

We decorated the walls of the large room at the back of the third floor, which we nicknamed the "war room," with charts and maps. Jenny prepared to lead our third training school in the large classroom on the fourth floor.

"How is this school shaping up, Jenny?" I asked, the week before the school started.

"It's looking good, Dave," she replied. "Most of the students are under twenty-five. One South African–born young man from Wellington is so excited about coming. He calls me almost every day. He can't wait to get here!"

"Sounds like the sort of guy we need," I said. "What's his name?"

"Grant Kelly."

I found myself remembering his name.

Soon twenty students arrived for the training school. Our twenty-two-year-old son, Joshua, was among them, along with four others his age, including Grant Kelly. Grant proved to be just as enthusiastic as his telephone calls had indicated.

Like most of our young staff, Grant had little financial backing and trusted God for financial support. To help pay for his training fees, he sometimes used the little free time he had cooking and selling sausages in local shopping centers, sharing his faith as he cooked. He spent many evenings at our home and soon became like an adopted son to us as we shared whatever was in our refrigerator and our family times with him. Grant was passionate about everything. Our eight-year-old son, Matthew, particularly looked up to him because they shared a strong love for cricket and enjoyed many hours playing backyard cricket together. They also spent long summer hours watching televised games of International Cricket, especially when South Africa was playing. Even Jenny, with laptop in hand, who had no real interest in cricket, soon joined the staff and students gathering in our lounge for the rowdy and uplifting times of fellowship during the One Day International Games.

Our volunteer staff continued to train throughout the preparation phase of the tour. In addition to classroom learning, they undertook on-the-job training in various aspects of tour preparation.

I walked in one day to our office, and our receptionist looked up and smiled as she answered the telephone. "Impact World Tour. Can I help you?" Behind her three young men huddled over a computer. The photocopier had printed out hundreds of copies of a letter I had drafted the previous day. Jenny and Jay were already in the "war room" when I entered. I noticed they both looked weary.

"What have you been doing?" I asked.

Jay had been up until after midnight working on youth discipleship with a small team. Jenny had been finalizing some details for counselor packs for the tour. In the background I could hear the rise and fall of voices in the office and intermittent telephone calls.

"This is a long way from your surfboard, mobile phone, and laptop, Jay," I said.

"Sure is," he said, grinning.

"Don't worry, we're nowhere near ready," Jenny said. "Dave, have you had a chance to review the Task Force manuals?"

I was thrilled at the hard work all of our staff undertook and the joy with which they served. Many of our staff and students left the security of their country, family, friends, and paid jobs. For some the cost was too great. One young man came from the USA to help with the database, website, and computer facets of operations. After a few days he realized the magnitude of the task and the sacrifice required by the staff. In an honest evaluation, he said, "I am not ready for this," and returned home.

A few received dramatic "guidance" to come to New Zealand. Just as dramatically they had "guidance" to leave. While this always grieved me, I was comforted by the story of Gideon in the Bible who started with a large army. Ultimately it was a very small number of soldiers who stayed and won the battle.

I realized that the inexperience of our staff did not hamper their genuine love for the Lord and their passion to serve Him. As General Booth, the Founder of the Salvation Army, said, "Only war makes veterans. Training and marching soldiers do not make veterans." General Booth sought to raise up veterans, not just people who lived within a comfortable framework without persecution and hardship of battle in the real world. IWT was not an easy, fun ride for adventure-seeking young people but was engagement in a real war for the eternal destiny of those outside of Christ. It involved a lot of hard work away from the limelight.

When the training school finished, our students left on overseas field assignments, working with IWT campaigns in Australia, USA, and Canada. My family went to the airport to say good-bye to Grant, who was joining the team in Lethbridge, Canada. I had no way of knowing as I embraced him, that I would never see him again.

While our students were overseas, we continued to lay foundations for the tour in the New Zealand church. Spurred on by the positive response of the Maori Gates Tour, I felt we also needed to honor the Christian leaders as we invited their participation.

It was a straightforward plan. First we were to share the vision with church, business, and civic leaders in each community. Then we were to raise the necessary finances and engage hundreds of volunteers in all the preparatory work. Finally we were to bring on the performing teams and promote discipleship of thousands of new believers.

Although the plan was simple, as a heated discussion arose in one of the early planning meetings, I realized how difficult it would be to impact the whole of the nation. Typical of our experience in meetings with church leaders was this visit to a town in the South Island. Initially all church and business leaders present gave a strong yes to embracing IWT.

But we were surprised during subsequent visits at how the questions arose. It indicated unease that lay beneath the surface. Demands of city lives and schedules made it difficult to gather all the leaders together to seek the Lord for His leading. Pastors who had not been at previous meetings found it hard to become involved. Many already carried huge workloads in overseeing their immediate church responsibilities.

"I heard that IWT hasn't done a good job working with and communicating with the churches," one pastor said. When I asked him more details about this, he had no real basis to come to that conclusion. I acknowledged that many of our staff were young and inexperienced. However, I was more concerned about the damage that this and other similar rumors could cause.

"We were offended by one of your top leaders," another said. I was glad that this had come out in the open, although the incident had occurred years before. When I approached our leader later, he immediately called and apologized.

"I don't think we are anywhere near ready in this town to take on such a large scale evangelistic project," said another more reserved church leader. While in one sense this was probably true, I always encouraged a response of faith to Jesus' command to share the gospel. Even He said, "*Do you not say, there are still four months, and then comes the harvest? Behold, I say to you, lift up your eyes and look at the fields, for they are already white for harvest!*" (John 4:35). It is only in seeing the harvest fields and going to work in them that we become ready.

This meeting certainly was not the positive enthusiastic response I had anticipated. I quietly prayed for the Lord to intervene.

"The budget seems far too high," someone exclaimed.

Oh no, I thought. In every town this was one of the most difficult hurdles to overcome, and we had already seen some towns not embrace IWT because of the amount of finances needed. Much discussion resulted on this point. Finally one prominent business leader stated, "There is a lack of united citywide vision and faith in reaching out into the community." He offered to personally raise half the required budget. The tone of the meeting immediately began to shift.

A Baptist pastor of a large church stood up and said, "IWT is an evangelistic arm of the church and can help us do what no one church can do. We need to get behind this." I noticed all eyes fixed on him.

With the input of the businessman and the Baptist church pastor, the meeting turned around. Soon we were actively discussing practical and spiritual strategies for taking the gospel into the community.

I noticed in this meeting that two leaders who grasped the possibility of impacting their community and who spoke out in faith were crucial in persuading the others in the room. Local leadership was essential to the success of the campaign.

In community after community, I was thrilled as some outstanding leaders took on the task of IWT. An Assemblies of God pastor in Gisborne felt so compelled to become involved that he said, "Even if I go alone, I'll go." One Auckland pastor stepped up to the task of leading the Pan-Auckland Task Force. While shouldering the demands of leading a growing church, he stood unswervingly by a conviction he received from the Lord. "I believe," he said many times, "that we will see more people come to Christ in 2004 than in any other year in our evangelical history."

One Christian leader who was initially opposed to the tour was challenged during a worship time. "I'll be there!" he sensed the Lord saying about the IWT Campaign, followed by a simple challenge, "Will you?" This leader immediately became involved in the tour preparation and enthusiastically mobilized others.

In Wellington, at one leaders meeting, a Queensland pastor who had recently hosted IWT and was visiting Wellington exhorted the leaders gathered: "First, make sure it is God's will for you to get involved. Second, get ready. Unbelievers came out like moths to the light to an event like this. There was a huge harvest in our town in Australia. We didn't expect such a response. We simply weren't ready."

Leaders in some towns eagerly embraced the vision of IWT and moved ahead quickly in preparation. In Tokoroa, a small country town lying at the crossroads between the lush dairy farmland of South Waikato and the vast plantation forests of the central North Island, a small group of pastors and leaders took only one meeting to decide that IWT was an opportunity for them. One of our facilitators was still driving home from the meeting when the leaders texted him on his cell phone, saying that they would be involved. Immediately he sent me a phone text saying, "Tokoroa is all go!"

Other towns were slower to come on board. We had made a few unfruitful visits to Invercargill, the southernmost city of New Zealand. Leaders were unsure of their commitment to IWT. Our staff continued to pray for this city.

Throughout the preparation stage of the tour Mark Anderson visited New Zealand every two to three months.

In Auckland, we visited Peter Ropati, a Sky Sports commentator, and marketing manager for Globe products, a company which produces skate-culture gear. After hearing the vision of IWT he was very supportive and offered the use of some skate ramps if we needed them. "I don't think anything this extensive has ever been done in New Zealand. It will be an absolute miracle if you guys pull this off."

As we climbed back into our van, I said, "He's right, Mark. It will be an absolute miracle!"

Mark grinned. "You just have to stick to the word of the Lord, Dave. Where is our next appointment?"

"We're meeting with our media director," I replied. "Then we have another meeting with business leaders. Tomorrow we leave for Christchurch. Over the next few days we will meet with church and business leaders and speak at some fundraising banquets and churches."

In every meeting, I observed Mark hold resolutely to the vision God had given him years ago for our nation. While he listened to criticism, he was never swayed by it. He always came back to the word of God and His purposes for New Zealand. Mark was the most focused person I had ever met.

After the whirlwind of activity during Mark's visit, I determined to do all that was possible to involve Invercargill. After a few more unproductive visits to Invercargill in the south, some of our staff tried to discourage me.

"I lived in the South Island for eight years of my life," I said. "I believe it is important that this city, one of the farthest geographically from Jerusalem, hears the Gospel through IWT.

It almost is the 'ends of the earth.' I have faith to believe this city will become involved."

As time went on, and many other towns and cities came on board, Invercargill seemed to move in the opposite direction. I encouraged our staff not to try to force people to get involved but to wait and pray.

Months went by. When we changed the tour dates, which would allow room for Invercargill at the end of the tour, I tried another approach. I suggested to one pastor whom I had known for many years that we just use Island Breeze, since the Maori leaders had shown a high level of interest during the Maori Gates Tour. There was still no advance. I had no choice but to leave Invercargill and press on with other cities as they prepared for the campaign.

"Lord," I prayed, "You'll have to bring this about. I've done all I can."

Some time later, I was surprised to receive a phone call from an influential Invercargill pastor, asking me if I would be willing to come down and meet with some pastors to discuss once more the possibility of IWT in Invercargill. Of course I was willing. Rearranging my schedule, I flew down as soon as possible and updated the small group of pastors and leaders who met together.

Eventually they decided to have two campaign nights with Island Breeze and GX. They even took an offering among themselves. With one of the church administrators assigned on the task force, they soon made up for the initial slow response.

Our staff in Auckland was thrilled when they heard Invercargill was involved.

"How did that happen?" asked Jenny, laughing.

"I'm not sure exactly what triggered the change, Jenny," I replied. "One thing I am sure of is that God is at work! The Invercargill guys are now in a place of faith and are making up for lost time!"

Some Said No

Some churches and communities chose not to get involved. Some already had excellent outreach, community, discipleship, and children's programs and did not feel that they either had time or needed to get involved. We recognized that it was not practical to draw everyone into IWT.

Some were resistant to what they viewed as imported overseas Christian programs. Some felt they weren't ready for a major evangelistic effort. Others felt that campaign evangelism was not for today.

One pastor said, "We don't have any skateboarders in our church, so we don't need this program."

A few churches struggled with what they felt was the worldliness of the IWT presentation, particularly the loud music. I lost count of the number of times I said, "It's not for you. It's for those who do not know Christ. Most of them have different tastes in music styles!"

Some thought the strong men were using supernatural powers. Others questioned how a skateboarding demonstration could be used to preach the gospel. In response to that criticism, I explained that God can use whatever skill we have, if we yield it to Him.

I think I heard almost every reason why not to get involved! Whenever we encountered resistance or lack of interest, apathy, indifference, busyness, objection to the amount of finance necessary, we always left that with the Lord.

Just as it had cost all of our staff in some way to work on the tour, there was a price to pay for all who were stirred to become involved. For those who took on the responsibility of task force involvement, there were the sacrifices of time and effort; for others there was the hidden cost of laboring in prayer. Others sacrificed finances.

I was soon to discover that among our trainee staff who were gaining experience with IWT overseas, one of them would pay a supreme price tag.

April 8, 2002

"David, it's Glen Smithson." I was surprised to hear Glen, who was overseeing the tour preparations in Lethbridge, Canada. I took the call in my office. Glen, usually bright-spirited and talkative, was uncharacteristically subdued. He came straight to the point.

"Grant Kelly has had a serious car accident. His vehicle was struck by an out-of-control car in the desolate Alberta prairie."

I swallowed hard. "Is he all right?"

"He's in a coma, fighting for his life. Get the troops praying."

Stunned, I walked into the main office area and broke the news to our staff. Right there we turned immediately to prayer. Prayer was quickly mobilized, not just in New Zealand but also in South Africa, where Grant was born, and Canada.

Over the next days, our main prayer focus was Grant's recovery. Glen kept us updated from Canada. Grant's health appeared to be improving. Our spirits lifted as we continued to pray.

Then at 4:30 AM on April 11, the phone rang. It was Glen. My heart skipped a beat.

"I'm sorry," he said in a voice that was grave, measured, but wavering slightly. "Grant's condition deteriorated rapidly during the night. Doctors were unable to resuscitate him." I groaned inwardly as I thought of the effect Grant's death would have on his family, our team, and all who loved him. Scenes of times with Grant flooded into my mind—the long summer evenings as he played cricket in our backyard, the friendship and laughter over meals and international sports, the times he had earnestly sought my counsel. Most of all I remembered his passion and intensity for those who did not know Christ.

Sue and I prayed in our bedroom until dawn broke. Our team members were stunned; the impact of losing a friend and brother, whom they regarded as a flag bearer to this generation, had a profound effect on us all.

I attended the Lethbridge Campaign the following month. At a "Heal Our Land" gathering, the night before the commencement of the campaign, a photographic tribute was shown on the big screen. Photographs of Grant as a young boy growing up in South Africa and New Zealand, right up until his time in Lethbridge, were shown. Many in the auditorium that night were moved as the chorus "Our God Is an Awesome God" played in the background and they remembered Grant, who gave his life in the service of God's Son. Hundreds of Christians from every denomination and background in the city passionately worshiped God as one.

Hundreds of young people responded to Christ during the campaign. One of the questions new believers were asked was, "How did you hear about the campaign?" At least one young responder simply replied, "Grant Kelly told me."

Shortly after Grant's death, our son Matthew gave a class speech entitled "My Hero." His clear, high-pitched, small boy's voice moved us to tears as he practiced his first-ever speech to a few of our IWT sports enthusiasts who continued to gather in our lounge room.

> Some people want Jonah Lomu or a famous actor to be their hero. But my hero was my friend Grant Kelly. He was twenty-two and always played cricket with me. He taught me some good bowling tricks and was always laughing and smiling. Sometimes he would joke with me. He went to Canada this year to tell people about Jesus. Sadly, he was killed in a car crash. When I grow up, I want to be like Grant and tell people in other countries about Jesus too.

Grant had touched us all in a similar way.

Chapter Six

Awake New Zealand!

Awake, you who sleep, . . . Christ will give you light.

Ephesians 5:14

Pressing On

While grieving Grant's death, we continued to press on with preparation. When we premiered the completed six-minute promotional video, our team members were all moved as they watched the scenic beauty of New Zealand portrayed against the background of Cindy Ruakere's appropriate song "This Is the Day." The video shifted gear into fast-paced action, bringing the reality of IWT closer. A short closing footage included a picture of Grant and a simple obituary—"You gave your all."

We used the video numerous times around the country, shown widely on *marae,* to civic and church leaders, to church congregations, and to fund-raising banquets, and it fast became a key tool in sharing the vision and inspiring the church of New Zealand to mobilize for evangelism.

In every community, I always looked for *advocates.* A lawyer from Tauranga drove the two-and-a-half-hour journey to Auckland to attend an information evening. Mark, who was speaking at the meeting that night, spoke on the need for advocates. The Tauranga lawyer understood that an advocate is one who pleads for another, or one who speaks in favor of a proposal. He became one of our many advocates.

One businessman in Tauranga approached me after a presentation in his church. I noticed tears in his eyes. He said that there needed to be a radically new and relevant way to convey the message of the gospel to this generation. But he had almost given up hope. His hope was renewed as he saw the scope of the nationwide vision of IWT.

Many other business people loved the big vision and the opportunities to use their organizational skills and resources.

To my surprise, the elderly were some of our greatest advocates. In many congregations, gray-haired folk indicated that they had come to Christ as the choir sang the well-known hymn "Just as I Am" during the Billy Graham Crusades. These were often the most enthusiastic advocates, despite the cultural differences between IWT and a Billy Graham campaign. "Our young people need this!" they said. Many of them formed a large part of the army of intercessors and helpers. In one church in Hamilton, the elderly baked cookies and went out of their way to invite youth and children to the evening events.

A Waikato Church Gets Ready

We were a small church, but IWT gave us something big to focus on. I was touched to see so many of

> my parents' generation and older take up the baton for IWT. They engaged in intensive prayer and were prepared to do long hours of hard work without recognition. They cooked, cleaned, served, and invited young people to their homes. Any generational gap diminished as we found common ground in Jesus. One woman who gave her life to Christ at the Billy Graham meetings in 1959 challenged us one night, saying, "I was one of those kids who went forward once, and I have never looked back. When those kids go forward, don't give up on them."
>
> *Hannah Peart, age 23, Hamilton*

Perhaps in the wisdom of years, when they recognized something God was doing, the elderly responded quickly and intuitively. Just as Simeon grabbed the infant Messiah and gave thanks to God, I encountered many in their 60s, 70s, and 80s who grasped this opportunity to be involved. Many saw it as part of a long-awaited answer to their prayers.

Faith

A group of seven gathered in prayer for IWT in a church meeting room. Some had been praying for twenty-five years for their small town. One said slowly, "Perhaps there are some obstacles in our lives holding back what God wants to do."

As she said that, the pastor was immediately convicted of his unbelief. "Lord, forgive my unbelief," he prayed.

Others in the group prayed for him.

With faith rising, toward the end of the prayer time, they all stood, held hands, and prayed, "Lord, we are willing to say yes to IWT."

Two people in the group, who had never given large amounts of money, felt they were to give generously toward IWT. Faith had been activated!

As I spoke in churches, I would ask those who had become Christians in the past two to three years to raise their hands. Sadly, in most churches I visited, very few people raised their hands. I noticed in my travels that there were many areas where Christians exercised a "survival faith," extending to their own family, health, finances, their own houses, business, and areas of interest. This did not seem to be expressed in active concern in a real and relevant way to impact their communities.

Perhaps the greatest challenge in the church lay in the spiritual climate and the level of faith exercised toward evangelism and evangelistic events. When asked on his 1959 visit to New Zealand about the passive role of the churches bringing religion to the people, Billy Graham replied, "It is an utterly tragic position when a church does not go out to the people. The Church must go into the world. The early Church went abroad. The believers went everywhere and bore witness. If a church does not go into the factories, the shops, the farms—if it doesn't go everywhere, it means that inspiration has been lost."[1]

Had the New Zealand church lost inspiration? Perhaps this reflected a lack of passion in our lives. Just as a marriage can lose love and become tired over the years if that flame of first love is not nurtured, our burning love for the Lord can fade while we go through the motions of faithful service. Would the Lord speak to the New Zealand church as He had to the Ephesian church in the first century? While He affirmed their hard work, their patience and endurance, and their hatred of those who were evil, He had one thing against them, "*that you have left your first love*" (Revelation 2:2-4). Were we in danger of "losing our lamp stand" (Revelation 2:5), that place of influence in the world, through losing our first love for the Lord?

One Auckland pastor believed that by the turn of the twenty-first century "a fog of disillusionment had settled over the church." He believed the Lord allowed this to bring humility and desperation in the heart of His people to seek God's way through this season.

Going Deeper
In Previous Generations

God has touched New Zealand with spiritual awakening in times past. Catalyst personalities have united the churches and helped to stimulate a measure of revival and harvest, bringing positive transformation to every aspect of national life. Witness, for example, the impact of R. A. Torrey's 1902 Dunedin meetings or the young Robert Laidlaw, founder of the Farmers Trading Company. When God's Spirit is poured out, the treasures of the land emerge, including a fresh generation of servant leaders who become the conscience and creative force of national life.

John Dawson

I felt that the church in New Zealand had, in some ways, entered her own dark age and needed, as the valley of dry bones (Ezekiel 37), God to breathe again on the bones as He had in times past.

One youth pastor, who had invested years of his life ministering to youth, said that things were darker now than twenty years ago. "We need a new wind of God's Spirit. We can't pretend that the methods of twenty years ago are having significant impact on our youth today."

Signs of a new wind of the Spirit of God were indeed emerging at the turn of the twenty-first century. I was encouraged by the bright spots in the New Zealand church and signs of Christian influence in society, which, I thought, if allowed to grow could have significant impact on our nation. Some growing churches, such as Auckland's Christian Life Centre (CLCA), regularly saw young people coming to Christ in their services. Christians around the nation were involved regularly in teaching Bible in schools, community outreaches, and children's clubs. Many were finding a new desperation in prayer. Others were activated into areas of prominence, such as politics and the media.

Strongly linked to youth culture is the foundation of music. Parachute Music Festival attracted an increasing number of attendees each year. Ben Lummis, the NZ Idol 2004 winner, echoed the sentiment of Christians working in other spheres when he said, "I want to use music as a vehicle to show people the God that is in my life in a relatable way. For so long Christianity has been boxed into the church. I want to take Christianity to the world outside the four walls of the church." Other New Zealand Christian performers, such as Brooke Fraser, or those with New Zealand heritage, such as British pop singers Daniel Bedingfield and his sister Natasha, were also making their mark on the world.

While traditionalists question some of the methods of these young performers as being worldly, I saw that this generation had to be reached with the gospel message in a way that was familiar to them. In previous generations, living for Christ meant belonging to a church culture that had little to do with trends outside the church. Today, however, a Christlike life is described more in terms of how we live and relate to others around us in love in the Spirit of Christ, without compromising biblical principles. There is always a danger of compromise, but that has always been the case.

Cardinal Williams asks the question, "Can we restore health and sanity to society?" The answer he gives is a strong but conditional "Yes." I add my yes to his—if we return to our foundational Christian values in this land. To do that, we must understand what those values are. We must preach the gospel in a way that is heard and understood, and live out authentic biblical Christianity in our daily lives. This could become one of the greatest challenges of the Western church in our day.

I understood the difficulty of some churches to become enthusiastic when so few were coming to Christ in their own churches. When I coupled that with the comparatively large outlay of finances needed, I understood their hesitation. I could only trust that as we shared the vision, the Spirit of God would stir people's hearts and touch them to sow by faith into a vision larger than themselves by giving their skills, time, finance, and prayer. Perhaps people wanted a larger vision. IWT was certainly a vision beyond the boundaries of every church, every community, and every region. I believed that if the church in New Zealand could embrace the national vision and see it worked out locally, it could have far-reaching effects.

For those churches that did rise to the challenge of hosting IWT, I observed a growing level of excitement and anticipation as believers worked together.

Going Deeper

Unity in Opunake

A local high school teacher in the town of Opunake, with a population of only 1,500, immediately grasped the vision for the youth. Some folk are third-generation beneficiaries. There were many relationship and drug- and alcohol-related problems. "Our children need this. We need this. We can do this!" she repeatedly encouraged other believers. When the local people raised all the finances for IWT, we knew this was a result of God at work in the community, so we set to work to make it happen in Opunake. Townspeople pulled together to provide hospitality with a willing and generous spirit. Local businesses sponsored newspaper advertising; Christians from all denominations began praying for Opunake with increased fervor. I have never seen such cooperation between Anglicans, Presbyterians, Pentecostals, and Catholics. As people worked and prayed together, there was an increased tolerance and respect for different styles of worship and a greater understanding of one another's differences. I saw, unfolding in our town, the blessing of God as a result of increased levels of unity.

Thelma Cuff

One pastor in a small town was amazed at the increased levels of unity in the lives of local believers. "The people of our town have never seen God at work in a coordinated way for a specific functional purpose ever before in their whole lives," he said.

A youth pastor was excited that people from his church who were not normally involved in church ministries became involved in IWT preparations.

I also found some stirring in the land toward a new thrust of evangelism. One church leader encouraged me, "It's time for a new wave of evangelism in the land." We believed IWT was part of this new wave. Paul Childers, leader of Awake NZ!, was also part of this new wave. After their twenty-two-week walkathon in 2001, raising money for Prevention of Child Abuse and preaching the gospel in towns and cities, Paul felt

New Zealand was one of the best mission fields. "We quickly discovered how ignorant of Christianity today's New Zealand youth are, yet how open to the gospel they are," Paul reported. "Young people yearn to do something! We can talk about youth in disapproving tones and the statistics are off-putting. But they want a life that will give them significance. If a whole generation of youth could be mobilized, New Zealand would change and have significant impact on the rest of the world! It's time to Awake New Zealand!"

I believed with Paul and many others in the land, that it was time to *Awake New Zealand!*

Chapter Seven

Where Does the Money Come From?

But without faith it is impossible to please Him, for he who comes to God must believe that He is, and that He is a rewarder of those who diligently seek Him.

Hebrews 11:6

"You'll never do it in New Zealand! You'll never raise over three million dollars for a nationwide evangelistic venture! It's so hard to raise finance for full-time Christian workers in New Zealand!" I heard these statements, or variations of them, in almost every town I visited. Where many churches struggled to survive financially and where the average per capita church giving each week was approximately twenty dollars per head, the unspoken message was, "Dave, you're crazy!"

In over twenty years of missionary life, Sue and I had experienced many extraordinary instances of provision. We also received faithful, regular, large and small gifts through the generosity of friends who believed in us. I was grateful for the confidence God had built in me that He was our source.

I had come to appreciate that it was not the *amount* of funds given that was important to the Lord but the obedience and faith in giving. After all, Jesus considered the widow's gift of two small copper coins, which she gave out of her poverty, to be worth more than the rich people's gifts, who gave out of their abundance.[1] Seven years in Singapore had increased my faith level. The release of finances we observed in Asia caused me to ask, "Why not in New Zealand, Lord?" I could only put my trust in Him, *Jehovah Jireh*, our provider, to generate the necessary funds.

One of the main strategies we used in raising finances was to invite interested people to a dessert banquet. I looked forward to a weekend in the small town of Whakatane, in the Bay of Plenty, where I lived as a boy. My family was with me, but I was not there to visit relatives or to relax on the beach. We were on a vision casting and fund-raising assignment.

I arrived early for the banquet and walked up the steps to the entrance of the Whakatane War Memorial Hall. Through the glass doors the flowers, fernery, and candles arranged carefully on the crisp, white tablecloths transformed the meeting room to a place of beauty and welcome. *I hope all those seats are filled,* I thought. A few people were milling about in the entranceway. Among them was our youngest team of facilitators, based in the nearby city of Tauranga, including our son Joshua. Joshua appeared at ease as he went over last-minute instructions for the evening with the task force leaders.

"Hi, Dad," he said, grinning. He introduced me to the Whakatane task force leader, a pastor from Ohope Christian Fellowship, and then turned to talk to the ushers. So, here was Josh, who initially moved reluctantly six months ago to Tauranga, now emerging as a confident young leader.

As the Whakatane pastor went over the program details with me, the hospitality team welcomed the arriving guests. The guests seemed representative of any community—parents, grandparents, teenagers, business people, education, and healthcare workers. Relieved and a little surprised, I noticed that all of the places were filled. Finding our places while last-minute light and sound adjustments were made, the dessert banquet was under way.

A local member of parliament endorsed IWT. A policeman shared some of his perspectives from dealing constantly with the "worst that Whakatane can give out." "I've visited murder and other crime scenes and seen some of the devastation going on in our community. IWT is an opportunity to lay hold of. We need to see a change come into the heart of our community, not just bottom-of-the-cliff rescue." One young blond task force member in a blue shirt could hardly contain his excitement as he described a vision he had seen years previously of the local football stadium filled with young people responding to Jesus Christ.

I outlined again the vision for IWT and God's leading for Sue and me to return to New Zealand. I shared how I felt the country was ready right now for a great harvest and that the spiritual tide was beginning to turn. I explained that even though some Christians had no interest in large-scale evangelism, this was in part how the early church began. The first sermon was preached by an uneducated fisherman as the Holy Spirit empowered him.[2] It was in the public place, and three thousand people came under conviction and responded to Christ. The church was added to and continued to grow by the preaching of the gospel.

God uses different tools for communicating His truth. IWT is like a hammer that breaks a rock.[3] It is a catalyst that speeds up the process of reaching the towns and communities with the gospel.

I gave a brief update of the communities around New Zealand that had already joined the IWT effort and were working hard in preparation. I outlined the three phases of preparation, proclamation, and preservation and described the tour content and showed the promotional video.

I invited those present to become involved, in essence, by giving, working, and praying.

As the ushers gave out the financial response forms, I explained the national and local costs, aware that the projected amount for the campaign in Whakatane was far in excess of any amount previously raised for a combined Christian event in the area. I suggested, as a basic standard for everyone, to consider pledging the equivalent of one week's wages over the next seven months before the tour.

A hush came over the room as the one hundred and fifty people contemplated whether or what to give. I sensed their genuine desire to give to the Lord through their resources. Some couples held hands and prayed together.

While some local and IWT staff counted the pledges and gifts, I also briefly outlined other ways the community could get involved. I suggested joining prayer teams or the growing volunteer work teams—of hospitality, ushering, arrangements, counseling, or follow-up. Again, people thoughtfully filled out the brochures.

The blond, blue-shirted leader handed me the piece of paper containing the total amount pledged. His beaming face conveyed the contents. "Dave," he said, his voice and faith rising to match his enthusiasm, "can we make it three nights in Whakatane?" As I announced that half of the total amount had been raised in gifts and pledges, unbelief dissolved in the room as spontaneous applause broke out. Although it was not possible to extend the time of the tour, I was encouraged by his response of faith, one which we saw repeatedly after the eighty fundraising banquets around the country.

The room looked empty as the banquet attendants left and the hospitality team packed away the table arrangements. I stood next to Josh and the two other young facilitators, as they finished packing their gear for the evening.

"Good job, guys," I said.

"Thanks, Dad," Josh replied. "It was awesome what happened tonight. These guys are amazing!"

Josh put some more envelopes in a box and closed it. "After working and praying with the people in these towns, I now know that God has called me to reach my generation with the love of God."

"Awesome, Josh." It was so good to see Josh and other young facilitators rise to a new level of responsibility for their generation.

"And, Dad," he added, almost cheekily, "make sure you're on time for the church presentations tomorrow!"

GOING DEEPER

Boost of Faith in the Small Town of Opunake

When the regional IWT facilitator shared with us that $8,000 was necessary for GX to come to Opunake, our faith failed us. However, he bolstered our faith with testimonies of budgets being raised in other towns. We set eighty places at the fundraising banquet, never really believing that all the places would be filled, and certainly not expecting $8,000 to be raised on that night. We were amazed when people from surrounding communities and farmlands turned up. Most of them were not regular churchgoers.

One of the TX performers also came to the banquet. As he blew up a hot water bottle, tore a telephone book, and broke a baseball bat, people seemed to understand that here was a tool that could help our young people. When the total pledged amount of $12,000 was announced, the room erupted into applause and loud cheers. Some, however, were still cynical. One older gentleman muttered under his breath, "Yeah, right!"

How amazed we were when the total amount of money even surpassed this amount!

This boosted our faith. It was all the proof we needed that God was at work in our community, and we set to work to make Impact World Tour happen in Opunake.

Thelma Cuff, Opunake

The morning after a fund-raising banquet in another small town, one of our facilitators pulled into a service station where his aunt worked. "I know most of those people who were there last night," she said, "and they don't have much money. You've seen a miracle!" She was not the only astounded participant. I was constantly amazed and touched by the beauty of believers coming together and giving sacrificially to a common purpose that would benefit their community.

During a pastors' luncheon meeting in Hamilton, two Tauranga pastors were also present. One shared some of the journey they had been on with IWT in Tauranga with finances and the growing unity he had observed in their city. "When Dave gave a church presentation one Sunday," he said, "I was staggered and a little envious that my congregation pledged $5,000 to IWT. We had so many needs ourselves."

"To my amazement," he continued, "our Sunday offerings have almost doubled since that time."

An Anglican minister immediately called out, "Dave, could you speak in my church next Sunday?" The meeting erupted in laughter.

We heard other reports of increased giving at this time as well.

People from the business sector also responded positively. "I don't know how you can undertake this enormous project at such low cost," said one business investor. He added, "I believe there are people in the community whom God has geared to invest in large projects, especially those with a strong evangelistic component. They think big and want to make an investment with return into the kingdom of God."

Compared with the cost of hosting the prestigious yachting America's Cup in New Zealand in January 2002 and the cost of film production of *The Lord of the Rings* and *The Last Samurai,* both filmed in New Zealand, the cost of IWT was really very low considering all that was involved.

We had expected to raise a large percentage through business sponsorship. We did receive some finances in this way, but most of the money came through generous individuals, where hearts had been awakened to reach those outside of Christ. It was grassroots giving at its best.

People also gave gifts in kind. Vehicles, food, equipment, business services, motels, ramps, materials were all donated and trimmed thousands of dollars from the budget. In a mix-up of communication, a pet-food company even donated pet food! Some local councils, such as Christchurch City Council donated finances. In Wellington, a scheduling clash with an international sporting event meant that we were able to use the Basin Reserve Stadium at a considerable discount.

As a large portion of the city budgets were raised, people rejoiced, faith increased, and hearts were touched to look outside of the church walls to those who had never heard of the love of Jesus Christ.

Businessmen Testify

As a committed businessman, I did not feel I could be physically involved in the tour, nor did we have any spare cash to give, as we were still establishing our business.

When challenged at the information evening for IWT, my wife and I felt we could give our services. We recognized that our area of expertise in helping companies to comply with Occupational, Safety, and Health requirements in New Zealand would be essential for IWT.

Almost immediately after the completion of the tour, all of our costs were covered through unexpected contracted work. We gave as unto the Lord and it seemed as though He rewarded us. He certainly is no man's debtor.

Brendan Woodnutt

For me, the IWT initiative was something that I was called to serve in and hence I was compelled to obey. God had brought me to a place in my personal circumstances which allowed me to respond relatively easily.

To be able to serve and give in obedience was a privilege, and then to see such immediate fruit from combined efforts was incredible.

Hugh Gollan

In Our Weakness

A few banquets failed dismally, such as one in Dunedin, where only the task force and a few others arrived. In such cases we were forced to ask some hard questions—were we relying on a method of fund-raising rather than the Lord and His leading? Had everyone done their homework properly beforehand? Had we become complacent in the light of the success of some other banquets? Did we involve the right people and work through relationships in the city in an honoring way? There was always opportunity for soul searching.

Slim, bespectacled Brian Kleinsasser, an American, brought much expertise as a qualified accountant as well as the experience of working on IWT campaigns previously. Still, there were many unknown variables and expenditures when it came to proposing a nationwide budget and breaking it down to local expenses.

I surveyed again the recent budget projections. "Brian," I said, "are you sure there is that much disparity?" The estimated early figure that we quoted to some smaller towns was, in a few cases, far short of the updated figure once the real costs of hiring and purchasing equipment were realized. I tried not to think about the reaction I felt could come from some of the task forces already working hard to raise the current figures. *This will really test our relationships,* I thought.

In my travels that week I had no choice but to humble myself and explain as best I could the reasons for the increase in budgets. Understandably, some leaders did feel a breach of trust. One executive task force had us sign a document stating that there would be no further increase in expenses. We did this, knowing that the eventual cost would increase more, but desired to walk in unity and keep to our word. I was thankful that most task forces understood and worked in faith and openness toward us to meet the extra expenses. Even in our weakness, we seemed to experience the Lord's favor.

Many resourceful New Zealanders thought that the local costs of the tour could be met at a lower price and that they knew how to do it. Some said so. "I'm sure we could cut a lot of expenses. We can hire some of the equipment here at a far lower price." One of the finance co-coordinators was being honest in the assessment of the projected budget. I appreciated the resourcefulness of New Zealanders. Out of our pioneering rural history I was struck with the thriftiness and willingness to innovate and make do with what was available. I admired Brian's patience in explaining the projected costs.

"You see," he would respond in such a confrontation, "you can hire cheaper equipment in your town at a cheaper rate, but we have to hire equipment for the whole tour. It has to be paid for up front before the tour starts. What is cost effective in your town is not cost effective for the whole tour." Once we sorted through national and local tensions, there was generally a respect and openness.

Testing Times

Although money was steadily coming in for our expenses, we had our testing times. If Brian was anxious about the looming deadlines for payments, his wry humor and patient spirit gave no indication.

November 10, 2003, for example, began as any other Monday morning—almost. Our usual morning prayer meeting in the war room began with an urgent $66,000 request. If we couldn't come up with that amount of money by 4:00 PM we would lose the contract on the technical gear. That would mean starting all over again, paying more, losing ground. We had only a third of the amount needed. I noticed Brian's index finger pushing his glasses over the bridge of his nose more frequently. Perhaps he carried more concern than he cared to mention. Still, I admired his dogged persistence and faith as he prayed, "Lord, You've brought us this far. You can't let us down now."

After examining our own hearts, we contacted city IWT leaders, making them aware of the pressing need. Some communities were able to pay part of their contribution toward national expenses. By the end of the day we were able to pay $55,000 and completed the remaining $11,000 a few days later as we had agreed with the contractors. We were certainly kept in a position of trusting God right up until the last minute!

Communities working together in unity and giving generously alone, however, were like two legs of a three-legged stool when it came to the preparation for large-scale harvest. We also needed the third leg, prayer, to be strong.

"To whom do I make a check out?" The gruff voice of the elderly gentleman towering over me surprised me. I had been invited to cast vision at a national gathering of Anglican Church leaders ministering in different areas of evangelism. My aim was to share the vision of IWT and to invite their participation where possible. I had not even mentioned the financial cost of the tour. In the course of our ensuing conversation, I discovered that the man had been involved in the Luis Palau Campaigns in New Zealand in 1987. He charged me authoritatively with the simple secret to the success of any large-scale evangelistic effort. "It's prayer, prayer, and more prayer." I could not have agreed more.

Chapter Eight

It's Prayer, Prayer

"If My people who are called by My name will humble themselves, and pray and seek my face, and turn from their wicked ways, then I will hear from heaven, and will forgive their sin and heal their land."

2 Chronicles 7:14

From the beginning we knew prayer was going to play a major part in the outcome of the campaign. At times we were overwhelmed with the brokenness of New Zealand and how far we had fallen from once being a predominantly God-fearing nation. We found a new "grace of godly sorrow," as Nehemiah and Daniel had,[1] as we considered the story of New Zealand. I had observed this godly sorrow in the early 1990s as many reconciliation initiatives took place.

During a tent meeting in Auckland, one person after another from the large crowd came to the microphone and confessed sins, hurts, and grievances. Preaching was put aside and humility engulfed the crowd as we confessed our own sins and those of our nation. We could not point our fingers in self-righteous accusation but only respond to the groaning of our own spirits as the Spirit of God moved among us.

This spirit of humility and reconciliation continued in localities around New Zealand. Representatives of churches and indigenous peoples gathered in different cities and wept and confessed areas of sin, particularly related to church divisions, abuse of authority, gender, and racial issues.

In many different settings, I witnessed again this grace of godly sorrow.

Jono Turner, a pastor and longtime friend, greeted me with red eyes the morning after he had been praying through much of the night. "I felt so grieved, Dave," he said. "All I could do was repeat the words, 'I'm so sorry, Lord. We have lost so much.' " Jono went on to lament the loss of so much of what he sensed the church had been entrusted with during the 1960s and '70s.

"We began to see the destiny and heritage of New Zealand emerging in those days of charismatic renewal," he said. "Many new things were birthed spiritually in those days."

We talked of *Scripture in Song,* the outpouring of the Holy Spirit, and the release of well-known teaching ministries throughout the land.

"And by the 1980s," I said, "New Zealand was the highest per capita mission-sending nation in the world."

"I believe," Jono said, "that we lost authority in the church that went with the inheritance of what came through the Charismatic Renewal because we contained it inside the church."

Many times our prayer turned into times of repentance. I found again that as we humbled ourselves and confessed the sins of the church and of the nation, we experienced a greater freedom in prayer. An important part of praying is humbling ourselves and grieving over the sins of the nation. It is in this place that we receive the grace of God and His heart for the nation.

Godly Sorrow

Godly sorrow is not the bitter weeping of a bitter spirit, not the condemnation of the enemy, not the regret over your besetting sins. It is the weeping of the intercessor.

It starts in private, grieving for the land and its people.

John Dawson

One morning in our small classroom, as we waited on the Lord for His direction, I felt compelled to read from Acts 8 about Philip going to the city of Samaria. As he preached the gospel powerfully, many individuals came to salvation and were healed and set free. Among them was Simon, a magician who held the whole city under his influence. As a result a city was set free from some major strongholds of witchcraft and sorcery. I shared with our staff and students that I felt that just as the proclamation of the gospel had helped alter the spiritual climate in Samaria and turn the tables in that city, the proclamation of the gospel across the nation could help turn the tide in New Zealand. In an unusual rising of faith, we declared that God would turn the tables in New Zealand, that this would once again be a righteous nation. We declared that every edict against the knowledge of God and His values would be overthrown. Jay put down his guitar and started overturning the desks in our classroom—enacting physically what we envisioned could occur in the Spirit. As books and belongings were scattered around the room, our faith rose to believe that God could begin to turn New Zealand back to Himself and heal the land.

Then, one of our American students exhorted us to never give up. Coming face to face with me, he began shouting,

"Never give up! Never give up! Never, never, never give up!" He was normally very polite, gracious, and self-controlled and apologized to me later for the forceful way he had shouted at me. I was not in the least offended. I needed this strong reminder to maintain the course of the vision.

The Ancient Pathways

> *"Stand in the ways and see and ask for the ancient paths, where the good way is, and walk in it; and you will find rest for your souls." Jeremiah 6:16 (NASB)*

During my vision-casting travels, an elderly, slightly bowed gentleman approached me and waited patiently while I talked with some others. Grasping my hand in a grip that I felt for days afterward, he said, "My wife and I have been praying for forty years for revival. I think we are starting to see part of the answer to those many prayers." In almost every town I visited, a small number of the elderly generation responded in the same way. In Foxton, a small group of mostly elderly folk had been meeting weekly for twenty years, asking God for revival. In Hutt City Covenant Fellowship, a prayer meeting had been going for fifty years, twenty-four hours a day. This prayer meeting was started in 1944 when the king of England, during World War II, issued a plea for intercession, and continued until 1994.

> ***Intercession is the real work. Service is participating in the results of the work of intercession.***
> **Joy Dawson**

We drew frequently from the wisdom and experience of Joy Dawson, a veteran intercessor and Bible teacher, who had helped to lay the foundations of Youth With A Mission through her intercessory lifestyle and teaching. Together with her husband Jim, Joy had been praying fervently for New Zealand on a weekly basis since 1956, many times with fasting.[2] Joy writes, "From the first time I heard about Impact World Tour, in 1999, near the inception of the vision, God graced my husband and me with an unusually deep burden for the fulfillment of this vision. I can only say that I have been compelled to pray with urgency, intensity, persistency, and strong faith."[3]

Others had also labored in prayer for New Zealand over the decades. During the two-year period that Campbell and Shelagh McAlpine were sent by God to New Zealand, Campbell fasted for twenty-one days, taking only water, with intensive prevailing prayer for revival. After this fast he led a small team of about seven men who were responsible for placing a Gospel of John in every dwelling place in the country. During that same two-year period, Shelagh and Joy Dawson met weekly to intercede for New Zealand and other nations of the world. Out of that commitment, the International Lydia Fellowship was birthed.[4]

Many other prayer warriors, now with the Lord, paid a great price in private, fervent intercession over many years for the country. These included Arthur Wallis, a Bible teacher and author from England. During the eighteen months he was in New Zealand, he, too, spent twenty-one days in prayer and fasting for revival. His wife, Eileen, prayed with him and ate only fruits and vegetables during that time. One of the six international leaders of World Evangelization Crusade, Rev. Ivor Davies, along with Dr. Greenway, a church leader in Hamilton, was steadfast in prayer for the nation. Muri Thompson, a Maori evangelist, who was greatly used of God in evangelism, also had a passion for revival.[5]

I realized that our generation owed a great debt to those faithful praying saints and others whose names we do not know. Any forthcoming harvest could be largely attributed to the labor of these saints from previous generations.

It is as if the prayers, tears, and prophecies for an individual, a family, a community, or a nation can be dormant for many years. In the right time the Holy Spirit activates them and brings alignment of people, places, and events to fulfill God's purposes in that area. The prayers are stored up in bowls until the overflow occurs, and suddenly things prayed for over many years occur with astonishing rapidity.

Yet we could not depend on the prayers of these prayer warriors alone. Our staff continued in daily prayer. I was amazed at the increasing number of prayer networks that were forming around the nation or were embracing IWT as a prayer focus. Intercessors for New Zealand, an organization founded in 1972 to encourage prayer for revival, the church, and the government in the nation, was one group that encouraged prayer for the tour. The 10,000 Christians living in New Zealand associated with Intercessors for New Zealand, together with approximately 450 in other nations, received their printed monthly magazine.[6] This included much insight as to how to pray for IWT and the nation during the preparation and proclamation phases.

In towns and communities where prayer networks and strategies were already established, it was a simple matter to include IWT within that framework. In Hamilton, Sue Rowe, a woman highly committed to prayer, helped initiate neighborhood prayer cells across the city. In the same city a prayer group met regularly at the stadium that would stage the performances. Prayer task forces in many towns, including Tauranga, organized forty days of prayer and fasting preceding the tour. Throughout the nation the Lord raised up an army of intercessors led by people whom the local churches in that community recognized as having the wisdom, authority, and gift to help facilitate the prayer focus for the campaign and the nation at large.

Sally Cowie, an intercessory leader in Christchurch, together with a growing number of leaders and intercessors, laid strong foundations in prayer for the campaign in their city. Regular prayer meetings were held in strategic places.

In Upper Hutt and Lower Hutt, a committed team of people who loved their city had already been involved in "Strategic Prayer Walking" at least three times a year for a number of years. Their strategy was simply to coordinate prayer walks with leaflet distribution for forthcoming events for the city, such as Carols in the Park and Parenting with Confidence. Praying for the forthcoming tour and distributing advertising leaflets in their city fitted in well with their existing prayer-walking strategy.

Strategic Prayer Walking

My three daughters (ages nine, seven, and five) and I have been prayer walking regularly in our area. As we delivered the IWT leaflets, we prayed for parents as well as kids to be affected by IWT. I felt led to pray for young boys without fathers and found strong emotion rising within me as I did so. My daughters and I see the prayer walk as a privilege, and we really enjoyed the time together, knowing that as a family we could have an impact on our city for God.

Paddy Smith (Upper Hutt)

To facilitate prayer coordination and communication, my personal assistant, Lexie Waters, e-mailed a weekly prayer update to the thousands of prayer volunteers around the nation, prior to and during the tour.

As the tour loomed closer, Operation Andrew was launched in most participating towns and cities. Inspired from the Bible story of Andrew inviting his friends to come and meet Jesus, this was a strategy shown to be effective in the Billy

Graham Campaigns and was adapted for IWT. Individuals were encouraged to pray for and invite five friends to attend the events. As seen in the Billy Graham Campaigns, most people who responded to Christ were invited by Christian friends. These new Christians were also more likely to be followed up, since a natural relational link had already been established.

One Auckland intercessor led teams of intercessors, by invitation, into some towns where Impact World Tour would be hosted. As they unobtrusively went about their business of prayer in Gisborne, Matamata, and Wellington, the Lord gave them specific instructions as to how to pray. Other small groups of intercessors prayed in strategic centers, such as local and national government centers or places where an unusual percentage of accidents or suicides occurred.

We were encouraged by reports both from within New Zealand and from other nations.

Prayer Concert, Perth, September 2003

After intense focused prayer for IWT in a prayer concert attended by over two hundred people, we sensed the following:

"We feel God will move mightily in the country towns and move like a bush fire on the cities and explode into them. The blessing is not just for New Zealand but for the nations. Australia is not to be excluded. We believe the fire will leap across the Tasman like a bush fire leaps across the road. Our confession to God is that we need what God is doing in NZ in Australia, and that together we would advance the Kingdom."

Peter Brownhill
Director, YWAM Western Australia

Jay, returning from a trip to the South Island, enthused over the youth prayer networks springing up. "It's incredible, Dave! All around the place young people are praying! They are on fire! In towns in the depth of the South Island, kids are laying hold of God and praying long hours into the night! It's awesome!"

"Great, Jay!" I said, encouraged by his report. "Everywhere I have been lately, I have seen an amazing surge in prayer. When God stirs His people to pray, you can bet He's up to something!"

I was amazed at the increase of prayer around the nation, but not just for IWT. I felt all kinds of prayer initiatives were increasing. Meanwhile, our growing number of volunteer staff put in long hours in both spiritual preparation and practical preparation for the tour.

Chapter Nine

Get Ready!

"Be strong, all you people of the land, ...and work; for I am with you," says the LORD *of hosts.*

Haggai 2:4

It's Your Turn!

By November 2002 many aspects of the infrastructure for the tour were in place with executive task force leaders forming in towns throughout the nation, while we were still working with some towns toward a definite involvement. At a meeting at Lifeway Ministries, many parts of the body of Christ joining together in the national venture were represented. This included Trevor Yaxley, the Lifeway Director, and his staff, all our New Zealand staff IWT leaders from other nations, and some chairpersons, pastors, and business people from different parts of the nation. I believe that the partnership between YWAM and Lifeway Ministries in spearheading the NZ campaigns, together with local churches and business people from around the nation, was a key factor in the blessing of the Lord in the preparation stages of the tour. Trevor came forward and shared the importance of what God was doing in New Zealand at this time.

"All over the nation right now, people are coming to faith in Christ. God works through whoever is available and obedient. IWT is here at the right time. People are needing to hear the gospel." Trevor had been a major advocate so far in the buildup of the tour, especially in the business community.

Mark emphasized the crucial role of proclaiming the gospel in determining the future of a nation. Cindy Ruakere, a Maori worshipper, led us in worship. She placed a NZ flag together with a Maori feathered cloak on the floor at her feet below the stage. Mark called people forward to lay down their lives in preparation for what was ahead. *What a privilege we all had to contribute our small part to God's overall purposes!* God's presence was there in a powerful way as young people came forward—some prostrate, some kneeling, and others standing in prayer.

During this meeting we commissioned our staff to go into three major cities—Wellington, Christchurch, and Tauranga—and to serve the smaller communities from these hubs. It was their turn now! They would now handle the bulk of the interface with local churches and continue to serve them in preparation for Impact World Tour. Other staff remained in Auckland, working on nationwide aspects of the tour, including media, finances, logistics, and discipleship. Some also worked on the citywide tour preparations in Auckland.

July 2003

Serving others serving others

We still had a long way to go to raise the necessary finances but had been encouraged by the response so far. Some towns were well down the preparation track; others were moving more slowly. One major concern was the area of transport. With six months to go before the commencement of the tour, all attempts we had made for a comprehensive transport package on a realistic budget had failed. Jay, Brian, and I had agreed together in prayer for the transport to come together. As with every other detail of the tour, we trusted the Spirit of God to release the right person, finances, and vehicles for this essential component of the tour.

As I talked with Andy Thornton, a down-to-earth New Zealander in his late twenties, based in Blenheim, I suspected we had found the right man for the job. His passion for jet boats and evangelism had lead him to establish Transport for Missions International, an organization committed to providing transport for missionaries in other nations. I felt his Transport for Missions motto, "Serving others serving others," was appropriate as he embraced our nationwide transport portfolio. "If you don't have transport, you don't have a tour," he pointed out.

True, I thought, *in addition to the many must-haves we were trying to put in place for the tour.*

As Andy, Jay, Brian, and I pored over tour dates, schedules, and budgets, Andy remained undaunted at the complexity of the task. "I love a challenge, Dave," he said. "I'll give this all I've got."

True to his word, Andy immediately obtained quotes from transport companies nationwide and was eventually able to materialize a comprehensive package, with excellent equipment on a minimal budget.

Despite the arduous task of putting the transport package together, Andy still managed to make time for his great love, jet boating. One day Andy invited our IWT facilitator Rachel Brown, her infant son Joshua, and me aboard his jet boat in the Marlborough Sounds, at the top of the South Island. The noise of the jet boat engine broke into the tranquil beauty of the attractive beaches and lush greenery as we sped along the intricate maze of waterways.

Rachel Brown was doing an excellent job serving the area and raising a baby at the same time. When a twig of willow flicked her nose while jet-boat skiing, causing a vivid flow of blood, I thought Andy displayed more than a brotherly concern for her. With each visit to Auckland, I noticed he talked more and more of Rachel and her son Joshua, and my suspicion that a romance was blossoming was confirmed.

Counselor Training

One of the most important aspects of campaign evangelism is to have trained counselors who know how to share their faith and to lead people to faith in Christ. With this in mind, six months before the commencement of the tour, we began preparing counselors in every community.[1]

Only 5 percent of Western Christians actively share their faith with unbelievers, yet we involved many ordinary Christians like Josie, a part-Maori plump woman from a rural area. "I really don't know what I'm doing here," she confided to one of the session leaders. "I've never talked to anyone about my faith in Christ." As Josie attended the training sessions, you could see understanding begin to dawn. The heaviness on her face lifted, and even the way she walked altered. She seemed to move faster, lighter on her feet. As Jenny led Josie and others through the message of the gospel, Josie began to understand with greater clarity God's purpose in creating us and that we all need to make a choice about how God has made a way for us to relate to Him through Jesus Christ.

During the second session, we showed counselors how to share their own testimony and use the *Real Life* gospel tract, designed especially for New Zealand audiences.[2] Potential counselors then tried out their skills during a mock altar call. After this session, Josie's confession had completely changed. "I now know that it's not just about believing in Jesus Christ but living for Him. Seeing Jenny, who is not a preacher, gave me confidence to think that I could speak to others about Christ also. That tract says it so clearly. I can't wait for the real thing!"

Thank You

I was amazed at how many people came up during the counselor training and thanked us for teaching them how to present the gospel. Some of them said that this was the first time they had ever heard the gospel presented so clearly.

Jenny Mollison

Others of the 9,775 people who attended the counselor training sessions throughout New Zealand echoed Josie's eagerness. Grandparents, housewives, teenagers, business people and professionals, teachers, students, and church leaders were all represented. For some, the counselor training was a refresher course; for others like Josie it was the start of a whole new way of life. All our staff who conducted numerous training sessions throughout the nation felt that this was one of the most faith-building and strengthening exercises in the lead-up to the campaign. An important part of the army was mobilized.

August–November 2003

Sneak Previews

Jason Hotere, a large Maori member of Team Xtreme International, returned with his family to New Zealand after seven years working on campaigns based in the United States. Rick Vanetta, a Canadian TX member, accompanied him.

These "big fat boys," as some of our team referred to them, helped prepare cities by running mini events in communities getting ready to host IWT. Between them, they blew up hot-water bottles, tore up telephone books, had human tug-of-wars, and shared the gospel at schools, combined youth events, churches, fund raising banquets, and one prison.

Some of the newly trained counselors tested their skills at small pre-tour events and had a taste of what would happen during the tour. In Wanganui and other small centers, so many people responded during pre tour events that there were not enough counselors.

Not enough counselors

Jason had the crowd eating out of his hand. He preached the gospel powerfully and when he gave an invitation to respond to Jesus Christ and live for Him, it wasn't just the young people that responded, but a couple of older folk as well. Four youth came forward who were also at the Youth For Christ Rock Solid Club on the previous Wednesday night. There were so many people coming down that we didn't have enough counselors.

Marty Emmet
IWT Coordinator

A taste of what is to come

We had an awesome weekend with TX in Blenheim and Nelson. So many youth turned up at combined youth services. It makes the hard work worth it, even when one person responds. It has given people a taste of what is to come and they are excited! Bring on the tour!

Rachel Brown
IWT Coordinator

In every place it gave the local organizers a clear picture of what the campaigns would be like as well as some hands-on practice. These mini-events put a face on IWT and brought the tour closer to reality.

Revive New Zealand

Another aspect of spiritual preparation was a series of Revive meetings, geared toward preparing the body of Christ for IWT. In October 2003 Joy Dawson addressed via satellite the five hundred or so gathered for Revive Christchurch. The message she received from the Lord summarized concisely the essential elements of spiritual preparation we had implemented in the build-up to the tour. She presented this message as an acrostic on the word IMPACT.

Going Deeper

IMPACT

1. "I" Imbibe, Impart, and Inspire.

We must first **imbibe** the vision for IWT, make it our own, and personalize it. We must **impart** and **inspire** others to go with the vision and run with it. God's intention is to ignite the nation with the flame of the Holy Spirit's fire and change the course of its history. *Ezekiel 20:47-48*

2. "M" Mobilize the body of Christ to be involved.

Starting with personal involvement to serve the vision of IWT and its purpose, we mobilize as many as possible. Joy strongly challenged those in Christchurch to get involved. *"I want to say to you dear fellow Kiwis and beloved Christians in Christchurch tonight: get on board this boat of divine purpose. It is a boat of historical importance."*

3. "P" Priority of Prayer—starting with the church.
Paramount importance of being filled with the Holy Spirit at all times.

4. "A" Always at All times be in unity. It's the source of our strength, and **humility** is the key.

5. "C" Call and Cry out to God to give each believer an increased burden for lost souls. **Commit ourselves** to intercession for the lost until the burden for lost souls grips our hearts.

6. "T" Train and disciple new believers to understand the character and ways of God, and to fulfill the Great Commission of *Matthew 28.*

Joy Dawson[3]

Many in the audience responded in a bid to personally apply the message.

After this meeting, the Christchurch preparation surged forward. Confidence increased as the fund-raising crew raised all of the finances necessary and as publicity materials arrived. By December, nine hundred volunteers had signed up to help out in the campaign. Prayer for the city increased.

In the War Room in our Auckland office, we all rejoiced as momentum increased in Christchurch, as we had prayed much for this city. The sneak previews, Revive New Zealand meetings, coupled with the logistical preparation, caused an increase in momentum, a buildup in faith, and a great deal of anticipation for the tour.

With the tour looming and the arrival of many new staff, we planned for all our staff to meet in Silverstream, near Wellington, in early December 2003. I was aware of the intense workload that many were carrying and sensed the need for refreshment and final instructions before the commencement of the tour. I did not realize at the time that this was perhaps the most important part of our preparation.

December 2003

Heart Preparation

We met for our staff retreat in a converted army barracks surrounded by bush-covered hills. Although it was officially summer, the cold, wet, overcast conditions seemed very wintry. I had not even met some of our staff who had come from all over the world to help us.

As I surveyed the room of approximately fifty weary but eager faces, I was thankful for all who had willingly come to join us in the work. "You've come from all over the place," I said, after the initial introductions. The many different accents conveyed the origins of some of our new volunteer staff from around the world. Staff from Germany, Ireland, England, Scotland, Denmark, USA, and Australia had come to join forces with those from New Zealand. "Thank you. Thank you for responding to the call to touch New Zealand for Jesus. We need your help."

On the surface, everyone seemed to be in good spirits. There was much laughter, and people enjoyed their free time together. Our staff gave excellent reports of what God was doing in the preparation phase in all parts of the country. All our staff testified to the wonderful provision of people, materials, housing, and transport. Despite the good spirits, laughter, and joy evident among our staff, I could not shake off an uneasy feeling that all was not as well as it seemed.

As Jay led the worship on Saturday night, I was strongly impressed with a greater measure of the fear of the Lord. IWT was *His* work. I did not want myself or anyone else involved to receive glory or credit for what rightly belonged to Him. Several team members expressed our need to humble ourselves before God. We had been entrusted with serving IWT and the body of Christ in New Zealand, but now, with so much of God's power about to be released, we needed to examine our own hearts.

Taubale Toki, a Fijiian brother who was working on part of the Auckland preparation, referred to the time when YWAM was seeking to purchase a ship in New Zealand. "The Lord showed Loren Cunningham that the ship had become a major focus and Jesus was standing in the shadows weeping.[4] It could happen again. IWT is only a vehicle for the Lord to use. Let's keep our focus on Him."

After Taubale spoke, silence engulfed the room. No one moved for what seemed a long time. Jay strummed his guitar in the background. Finally one girl came forward. "I've had so much pride in my heart over IWT," she said, her voice breaking slightly. "Please forgive me. Please forgive me, Lord." She could have spoken for many of us. Others of our staff were quietly praying in agreement.

One at a time, many of our staff took the microphone. One confessed areas of hurt in a relationship. Others were convicted of putting work for the Lord in a position of greater importance than our love relationship with Him.

Dutch-born Frank Eijgengraam shared how he had come to the end of himself and close to burnout in handling the immensity of the logistics of the preparation phase. "I had to learn to trust God in a deeper way," he said, his slight Dutch accent showing through. "At the end of the day, I had to put aside the pressures and worship God. I had to rest in the midst of pressure. I had to put God in first place, not my work for Him."

For all of us, it was easy to become swamped with preparation details such as corporate prayer meetings about IWT and the city, meetings about discipleship, teaching about the gospel, writing letters of vision and encouragement, and speaking about the harvest that was to come. God's work, even something so much on His heart for us, could easily take the place of our personal relationship with Him. We realized that IWT really was all about God and what He was doing in the nation. If we maintained our love relationship with Him, He would take care of all the details of ministry. We had to have our relationship with God in first place.

I stood and tore up my name card as Director of IWT New Zealand, symbolizing that I desired to see the Lord's Name and glory through this ministry, not my own.

As the evening progressed, our staff humbled themselves and shared personal areas of their lives. Some shared areas of personal struggle, even of failure. Tears and laughter flowed in an atmosphere of love, humility, and acceptance of one another. We realized that this openness, humility, and posture of putting God first in everything had to be lived out daily, not just for this one weekend. That included our relationships.

With the influx of many young recruits, and recognizing that the forthcoming months of the tour would be intense, I discouraged our team from forming new romantic attachments during this time. "After the tour," I said, "that's a different story. If you sense the Lord leading you in a romantic relationship, you'll find each other. These next months are full-on battle zone. You won't have much time for developing new relationships."

We had seen deep levels of unity and humility in community after community around the country, as local believers embraced the challenge of IWT. I realized that we had to apply the same litmus test to ourselves as the Holy Spirit shone the beacon of His searchlight into the shadows of our hearts. I felt that the honesty we shared that night bound us in stronger love and greater liberty than we had previously known. It did not mean that all our struggles were resolved, but we had personally experienced cleansing in our hearts and knew for sure that we could not take any of God's glory for ourselves. I felt a load lift from my shoulders. IWT staff were ready for action. Let the tour begin!

Outcomes: Preparation

- International, national, and local prayer mobilized
- Local executive task forces formed in 50 centers
- Resources in-kind and **$4.4 million cash raised**
- 500 YWAM and Lifeway Army personnel as staff, crew, and support
- National television and radio media campaign
- Transport fleet organized
- Stages, performance ramps, and sound and light rigs set up
- Approximately 2,000 decisions for Christ during buildup events

Outcomes: Church Participation

- 500 local church presentations
- 15,000 volunteers
- **5,000 pledges from financial supporters**
- 1,500 church-based discipleship programs registered
- 93,000 Operation Andrew prayer cards distributed
- 9,775 first-contact counsellors trained
- Generous hospitality for teams

Chapter Ten

The Tour Begins

January 2004

The two hundred performing team members and technical staff came from all over the world—Brazil, Egypt, Holland, Denmark, Pacific Islands, USA, Canada—and from New Zealand. Ray and Shaneane Totorewa had gathered a team of thirty-eight Pacific Islanders and Maori from around New Zealand to join with the International Island Breeze members. Dancers, rollerbladers, strong men, and cultural dancers all converged in Auckland with a desire to make a difference! Most paid their own travel expenses. Excited teenagers joined with experienced athletes and performers of Impact World Tour.

As the teams spent long hours training, preparing, and practicing for the imminent tour, our preparation team worked on all the last-minute practical details. Jay was still working on the ramps. An events management team from Australia set to work finalizing arrangements for Auckland venues. Andy Thornton finally organized a fleet of Nissan Safaris to complete the transport package.

I shut the door of my office, closing out the incessant telephone calls and frenetic activity of our office staff and volunteers as the logistical preparations reached fervor. Brian and I again sat down and began praying how to meet another payment of $66,000 for the technical gear in addition to the other bills that were mounting. This time we were comforted from Matthew 6:34, "*Do not worry about tomorrow, for tomorrow will worry about its own things. Sufficient for the day is its own trouble.*" We felt we were to pay today's bills and not worry about tomorrow's. I wrote out the checks for the bills for that week and trusted God with Brian for the remainder of the finance due the following week. We were confident that the remainder of the necessary dollars would come from the cities.

That day, the burden of wondering where money was coming from and whether we would be able to pay all the bills was gone. We came to a place of confidence that God was not just providing—He was our Provider. He had moved people's hearts throughout the preparation phase to contribute through their finances, their resources, their skills, and their abilities. I could only trust that the miraculous life-giving power of the seed sown during the preparation time had gone to work and that a harvest would be reaped.

January 17, 2004

Mark Anderson and I joined the two hundred gathered in the YWAM training center courtyard in South Auckland, near where I had first agreed to undertake IWT in New Zealand. As the athletes, performers, and support crew gathered for the final days of preparation, orientation, and teaching, I could hardly believe that the dream Mark and I had shared three years ago was about to become reality. Three years of intense preparation culminated here. Yet it was just a beginning.

During the last morning of our preparation time, everyone involved began praying, some in groups, some standing alone. It started quietly. Soon there was a roar rising from the courtyard that sounded like surf breaking in a wild storm. Young people were overwhelmed with the presence of God. All around the courtyard people were praying for one another, for the nation, for a visitation of the Spirit of God, and for many to come to the knowledge of Christ.

It did not stop. Over the next three evenings, Loren Cunningham, John Dawson, and other leaders ministered at a series of meetings in central Auckland called Revive New Zealand. Capacity crowds gathered in the summer heat. Worship teams from Auckland city churches helped usher in the presence of God. Without consulting one another, each speaker referred in a different way to Isaiah 60:1, *"Arise, shine; for your light has come! And the glory of the Lord has risen upon you."* Each felt that this was a unique time in the history of New Zealand and exhorted us to rise in faith. On the final night, Cindy Ruakere's song "This Is the Day," which we had used on the IWT promotional video, came alive in this context. Jay led a spontaneous *haka* (rhythmic Maori war dance). The room erupted in praise, applause, and prayer.

Sandwiched behind the team of performing artists and athletes, I joined the mass of warm bodies that reached out to pray and commission the teams to their task of preaching the gospel of Jesus Christ around the nation. Loren Cunningham's rich voice boomed across the rising volume of prayer. "We commission you to the task of evangelism in New Zealand!" He exhorted authoritatively, charging the staff and teams with Mark 16:15, "Go into all the world and preach the gospel to every creature." IWT was launched!

Despite the groundswell of prevailing prayer, the enlisting of thousands of prayer warriors, and the unity brought about by citywide prayer meetings, I could not shake off the feeling that there was still another dimension to prayer that we needed. Even as we began to see evidence of the Holy Spirit moving in the boot camp and Revive Auckland gatherings, I still felt there was much more to praying than we had as yet experienced.

"Mark," I said at the conclusion of the tour launch, "it is as though IWT is the tip of a sharp arrow, but the tip is not fully formed yet. There is something missing."

I did not know exactly what that was, but as the tour commenced and we engaged in some intense spiritual battles in our faith journey, I soon discovered a whole new dimension to prayer.

JANUARY 19, 2004

...AND MORE PRAYER

"Dave, it's Mark." I had already received many calls that morning, as last-minute arrangements still needed sorting out for the commencement of the tour in two days' time in Gisborne. When Mark called from Gisborne, I was expecting to confer with him on numerous tour details that needed attention. I was surprised to find his tone of voice subdued, his speech almost slurred. Mark related how he had awoken that morning with a strong impression of waves breaking onto the shores of New Zealand and young people fanning out into Asia, the Pacific Rim, and the rest of the world.

"Sounds like Loren's initial vision in the birthing of YWAM," I said, wondering where Mark was going with this conversation.

"Exactly," he said. "I have been awake for hours this morning, with a profound sense that God desires again to send waves of young people into the nations, proclaiming the love of Jesus. At the same time I feel the jealousy of the Lord for

New Zealand and the church here." Mark paused, as though gathering his thoughts to express in words the essence of his encounter with the Lord that morning.

Later that morning in a conference call with John Dawson and Mike Bickle, the founder and director of the International House of Prayer (IHOP) in Kansas City, Mark and John relayed their sense of importance of the New Zealand Impact World Tour to Mike. Aware of the need for more prayer for New Zealand during Impact World Tour, John asked Mike and the IHOP to consider undergirding this project in prayer.

"It's as though God is aligning two organizations with different emphases for this tour. IHOP has emphasized day-and-night prayer and worship for the nations since September 1999, coming from the believer's intimate relationship with the Lord. Combining that prayer focus with IWT in a commitment to proclamation evangelism, together with the groundswell of prayer in New Zealand over generations, could result in a powerful synergy!" he said. "Anyway, Dave, I will update you after my visit to Kansas City next week. I believe God is orchestrating and aligning people in ways that we never imagined!"

The Tour Begins

> *"Put in the sickle, for the harvest is ripe.... Multitudes, multitudes in the valley of decision! For the day of the Lord is near in the valley of decision." (Joel 3:13-14)*

Gisborne

The first city to greet the sun every day

Two hundred or so local Christians gathered at the newly constructed Breakthrough Church for the IWT Harvest Celebration, in this first city in the world to see the sun every day. Ordinary people testified as to what God had done in their lives as they had worked together during the preparation phase of the tour. People rose to positions they would never have taken up if not for the leadership of Gary Stephenson, an Assemblies of God pastor, who led the charge. His steadfastness and confidence helped inspire others. He shared what an amazing experience working in preparation for the tour had been and the grace of God he had experienced. Others quickly jumped to their feet and testified. One woman who coordinated some of the best home-cooked meals New Zealand could offer, enthused about her experience: "I got to meet and make friends with some awesome people. It was a huge blessing how many churches from Gisborne worked together. I saw God do miracles. Just when I needed help, He came through in amazing ways! Thank you for this experience."

What a contrast to that first meeting when Gary Stephenson had stepped forward in saying yes to the tour!

Mark exhorted those present to return to biblical Christianity and to be prepared for what God wanted to do in the land. Many prayed accordingly as they dedicated themselves afresh to the Lord and to this time of harvest.

The following night, the first campaign night of the tour, I attended the prayer and counselor briefing, held in a local school hall near Awapuni Stadium. The room was full of local believers armed with *Real Life* New Testaments and tracts. I was overwhelmed with God's presence and sensed some of the joy He must experience when His people come together in unity to reach out in evangelism. As I looked around the room, the counselors listened attentively and prayed sincerely. I sensed quiet anticipation among them, coupled with a degree of nervousness.

As I walked along the Wainui beachfront to the stadium, the music blaring from the loudspeakers masked the breaking of the waves. I could hardly express my gratitude to the Lord for bringing us to this point. As I entered the open stadium, some of the crowd was already seated on the sloping grass areas. Young people, families, and individuals were streaming into the stadium. A large proportion of the crowd were Maori. I prayed, "God, draw them to Yourself."

Ominous rain clouds gathered over the distant hills, a warning of the conditions we were to encounter over the next month. TX members bounded onto the stage as the excited crowd cheered them on. IWT was under way.

"We're a group of Christian athletes from different countries who have come to share the message of Jesus Christ with you. We're not here to show off. We're not here to just entertain you. Everything we do has a meaning and a purpose." The purpose and meaning was clearly presented as one after another TX International members briefly told their personal story of how Christ had changed their lives.

I could almost feel the Holy Spirit drawing pain from the heart of the crowd as one young man told how he had been raised in a home where fear pervaded due to his father's unpredictable violent outbursts. The fear was replaced with rejection and abandonment as a court restriction had to be placed on his father. He explained his own resultant anger and hatred, which only disappeared as he reached in faith for the love of God the Father expressed through Jesus Christ. "He is not like any father on earth. He will never hurt you."

As the strong men graphically broke more stacks of bricks, representing the sin in our own lives of anger, violence, selfishness, pride, rejection, and hurt, I winced as I sensed walls in the hearts of many breaking down. I felt that hope rose in members of the crowd as TX members told their stories of overcoming despair through faith in the living Christ.

Video clips on a huge screen interspersed between the strong men's acts were alternately humorous, then serious, at one point displaying a clip of Jesus dying on the cross. Even when the rain came down, the enthusiastic crowd remained under cover of their umbrellas to watch the show.

> **IN A NUTSHELL**
>
> ***This is what is written: The Christ will suffer and rise from the dead on the third day, and repentance and forgiveness of sins will be preached in his name to all nations, beginning at Jerusalem.***
>
> **Luke 24:46-47 NIV**

As Jason Hotere strode onto the stage, his long hair flowing, his brown skin rippling over his muscles, a hush came over the crowd. He greeted the crowd first in Maori, then continued in colloquial English. "You gotta be proud, Maori people. You gotta be proud, Islanders. You gotta be proud, Pakeha, of who you are." He shared from his heart how God, in Christ, had come into his life. He had grown up in a family where there were struggles with anger, alcohol, and violence. Soon he turned to bullying and began to repeat the cycle of aggression.

When his girlfriend left him, he felt depressed, alone, and unloved. He was close to the point of suicide. Late one night, his friend Josh called him.

"Uh, Jas, it's Josh here. I felt I should phone you. Uh, do you like, need anything?"

How could he have known I wanted to take my life? Nobody knew. "Mate! What made you call me?"

"Well, Jas, I was about ready for bed and I felt like God told me to call you."

"That freaked me out. I soon did a 180-degree turnabout, and God started to change my life."

Jason continued to share in his own words how this "crime-ridden Maori fella" was given a destiny, a hope, and a future since his life-changing encounter with Jesus Christ. Not only had this encounter changed his life and given him purpose, hope, and a future but also that of his young daughter, whom he picked up and gently held in his arms. That spontaneous act of picking up his child and seeing the little girl safely in her father's embrace illustrated a hope and future for the coming generation. The curse of past darkness over his family was now broken. More concrete blocks were smashed to demonstrate the fact that Jesus Christ breaks every sin and bondage over families. Jason gave the appeal for all those who wanted Jesus to take control of their lives and to have the walls of sin broken down through the death of Jesus.

I could hardly believe the number of people who started moving quickly forward even before Jason finished speaking. Counselors stood behind them as the altar call and prayer continued. Walking among the counselors, I heard the gospel clearly explained as tears fell, Bibles were given out, and details were taken for follow-up.

> *"I think it has been the presentation of a clear gospel message. It's the truth; it's been presented well, the people have grasped it. They'll grab the truth and the truth will make them free! The people that came up to the altar call, it was noticeable that they understood the message, and you did not have to convince them to make a decision."*
>
> *Pastor Gary Stephenson*

Second Night (Island Breeze)

The Grace and Mana of the Pacific

The fact that I couldn't find a parking place anywhere near the stadium indicated that things were looking good. What a cultural banquet the three thousand people who filled the grandstand and the grass in front of the stage were about to receive! The first performance set the scene for an outstanding demonstration of the richness of Maori and Polynesian culture. The show opened with an audio piece with haunting sounds of the land that was then shadowed with the spoken word of God from John 1:14, first in Maori and then in English. It was followed by a Maori act, performed with such strength and grace that it won over the hearts of the crowd. The Samoan acts brought the Samoans to their feet. Enthusiastic Samoan shouts echoed through the stadium. The fast-moving fire dances were breathtaking indeed. The Tongan acts displayed great joy. Tahitian and Hawaiian acts brought colorful entertainment as well as joy. The smiling faces of the dancers were well displayed on the large video screen as the cameraman focused on them.

Again, interspersed throughout the performance were personal testimonies from team members who told how Christ had transformed their lives.

I could almost smell the steak and sausages that Kimiora, a young Maori man, cooked as he chatted about real life and family struggles on the huge video roll-in, interspersed in short three-minute segments throughout the evening. Again, everyday issues, language, and humor struck a chord with the crowd. He shared how he had grown up going to church but questioned the traditions, why he had to dress up, why people gave all their money to the church, and was told, "That's just how it is, bro." When things weren't working well for him, he "got to thinking about that Jesus stuff." "What was so bad that God had to send His only boy to fix it?" Kimiora shared his own New Zealand worldview. "I'm really a good fella. I've never murdered anyone or stolen anything." His friend explained to him that God's rules were given in love for us and to protect us from being hurt. He reflected on how hurt he had felt as a father when his daughter cut school and lied about it. He realized that he had a feeling deep inside of needing something, and that emptiness would go away for a while but was never satisfied.

Maybe we did all need Jesus. "Even my nana told a few lies."

"I was ready to give it all over to Jesus." Then his friend told him to think it over first.

The pace quieted as the Maori dancers again came on stage. Ray Totorewa, dressed in Maori warrior's attire, came on stage with his slim, blonde Australian wife, Shaneane. "In every culture you can see the fingerprints of God," Shaneane said. "One of the most obvious signposts I see in Maori culture is the acknowledgment and honoring of God as the Creator." She went on to share from her heart the beauty she saw in the Maori people and honored them.

I noticed the groups of Maori people sitting on a rug near me nodding their approval.

A medley of traditional Maori songs highlighting different regions of New Zealand followed. For the first time, Island Breeze had included in their dynamic cultural display a stage presentation that was specifically designed to reach Maori, including the opening Maori acts, the Kimiora video roll-ins, Shaneane's honoring piece, and the traditional Maori songs.

Rudy Valle, a Hawaiian leader of Island Breeze, clearly presented the gospel. Rudy shared his own testimony, highlighting the importance of expressing the beauty, potential, and purpose of each culture, but emphasizing that Jesus is the "true essence of life."

Ray Totorewa then came on stage in warrior's stance and symbolically placed a *wero* (challenge) at the feet of the crowd. Rudy explained the challenge that God places before us—to choose life in Christ or an eternity in hell. Again, as he gave the altar call, people streamed forward. I noticed a number of families responding and many Maori and Polynesian people.

When I went backstage afterward, Ray and Shaneane were surrounded with brown-skinned people touched by the Maori elements of the presentation. I caught Ray's eye and gave the thumbs-up sign. His face beamed with satisfaction. They had responded in faith to God's heart to honor the people of the land and subsequently put together a relevant presentation. I rejoiced with them as they experienced the joy of seeing some immediate results of their hard work.

Third Night

GX International

The largest crowd for the three nights gathered for the final night. "Our God is a fun God!" declared Nate, the young evangelist, as he rolled around the skate ramp. Amidst cheers and cat calls from the crowd, he introduced other skaters and bladers, Thomas Hansen, a former BMX World Champion from Denmark, Jesse Fellers, already a veteran GX evangelist in his late twenties, and his younger brother Sierra, who had won the International Amateur Skateboard championships in January 2004.

From then on was a stunning array of skill, loud music, a blur of action, of rap, break dancing, dancing, video clips, and testimonies of young people and their deliverance from lust, suicide, drugs, hopelessness, despair, and loneliness. A young dancer from Wellington was still recovering from the shock of his sister's death after she had inhaled the contents of a spray can. From firsthand experience, this young New Zealander could share the devastating effects of teenage experimentation with drugs and alcohol.

After each act, the young crowd screamed for more. But even with thrilling, hair-raising action, young people were moving about the grounds and stands, texting one another and calling out to their friends. The restlessness of this generation gripped me. *Only relationship with You, Lord, can provide what they are searching for. Do for them what You have done for me,* I continued to pray while the blur of action continued.

Going Deeper
Restless GXers

The GX crowd is typically restless, moving around, texting, multitasking, chattering among themselves. As you look out on them it is like a restless sea of humanity. This generation seems to be a fatherless, somewhat abandoned, and independent generation. I consider the restlessness an indication of their soul, that as it is for the heart of every human being, the hearts of these young people crave peace. The kids identify with the fast-moving skateboard and dance culture and their attention is riveted by someone who speaks their language and reflects who they are. They are relieved to hear truth spoken without frills. They relate to lives that are similar in culture to their own, that are familiar with the pain and separation they have experienced, yet can give hope and purpose through a dynamic relationship with Jesus Christ. If you earn the respect of this generation, they want to hear what you have to say. They are looking for answers.

Jesse Fellers
GX International skateboarder

As Jesse put aside his skateboard and clearly presented the gospel and shared his own testimony, I felt the crowd settled slightly. He used the words heaven and hell, explained that

God's design for sex is best expressed in a marriage relationship between one man and one woman. He finished by giving a clear and precise altar call, calling those whose lives were messed up with gang connections, and those in wrong relationships who were bound and feeling condemned to come forward. I watched the crowd become quiet, and young people come forward under the conviction of the Holy Spirit.

Testimonies

My sons wanted to see Island Breeze

"I only came because my sons wanted to see Island Breeze. I came forward at the altar call because I knew I needed to rededicate my life to Jesus. Life has been hard, and I knew I needed to forgive. I had hardness in my heart that could only be released through forgiveness. As I prayed and cried, I began to experience God's wonderful love. I have some issues I need to walk through, but I am not alone anymore. God is walking with me."

Two young women

Two young women, both pregnant and not married, came forward. They both wanted to get right with God.

Counselor

The whole family

A boy came on Island Breeze night and committed his life to Christ. The following night at GX night, his mother committed her life to Christ. On the final night, TX night, the father also received Christ.

All her grandchildren

One praying grandmother rejoiced as all eight of her grandchildren responded during different evenings to the gospel message.

It's just so awesome to be blessed that God has answered many prayers

One woman, who had had a hard life experience of drugs, gangs, and attempted suicide, was weeping at the altar call. "My heart is weeping, as I look around and see all our young ones. As I was growing up, all I wanted was someone to put their hand on my shoulder."

Not just the young

Brahm, a Dutch member of TX, went into the crowd after the performance as he noticed a Maori woman in her seventies who was unable to walk to the front during the altar call. He prayed with her as she surrendered her life to Christ.

Chapter Eleven

The Tour Continues

During the next three weeks, as the tour moved through the small towns of the lower part of the North Island, the gospel continued to be preached in simple, vibrant, and relevant ways. In every one of the small towns, people responded to the timeless message.

In Opunake, which has a total population of 1,500, expectation of the Christian community culminated as GX arrived in town. The teams were hosted at Parihaka Marae at the base of Mt. Taranaki, the mountain made world famous by the recent film *The Last Samurai*. This area was of historical significance during the Maori land confiscation during the 1840s. Many of the youth associated with the marae were impacted by the stunning performances of the GX team. Perhaps an even greater impact was left by the authentic lives of the GXers as they related with the young people.

Thomas Hansen, evangelist and world-class BMX rider from Denmark, prayed for a teenage girl on crutches. She discarded her crutches and plaster and was completely healed.

In nearby Marton, crowds jammed the local Memorial Hall. Some even climbed the fire escape for a better view, while others stood on chairs or spilled over into the aisles. One pastor commented that the crowd coming out for TX was the largest gathering to hear the gospel in the twenty-five years he had been there. Another remarked that he saw people at the campaign nights whom he knew had never been involved in church before. He said, "This is reaching out into the community where it is needed and giving people an opportunity to hear the gospel in a relevant way."

I watched "some from the community" responding at altar calls. Gang members and weeping teenagers were among them.

It's Worth It

As I was standing at the altar call watching people go forward, tears were filling my eyes and I was saying, "Yes, Lord, it's worth all the money, it's worth it! I've never seen a hall full like this for any event in Marton. My advice for other places still getting ready is pray! Work hard together! Be prepared to take a risk, take a gamble, and take a step of faith."

Phil
Hospitality and Publicity Chair for Marton

Two youth leaders from nearby towns dared high school teenagers to come to Wanganui, Marton, and Hawera and see for themselves. Thirty young people on one bus came forward at an altar call. The other youth leader started a whole youth group with those who indicated their acceptance of Christ.

I was inspired by these youth leaders, who did not listen to a widely held opinion that this generation is not interested in the gospel and will not respond. They went to great lengths to get nonbelievers to the tour. I urged all those involved in towns where the tour was coming to invite as many nonbelievers as possible.

> **Please Keep This Focus**
>
> ***The secret is bringing as many nonbelievers as possible, not just Christians coming as spectators. IWT is for the lost, and where the church is geared that way, fruit is coming. Please keep this focus—toward the lost.***
>
> **From David Cole's Weekly Update, Jan. 31, 2004**[1]

In Hawkes Bay, situated on the lower eastern half of the North Island, it was wonderful to observe the two sometimes rival cities of Napier and Hastings working together, along with nearby Havelock North. As thousands of visitors to Hawkes Bay during the Harvest Weekend sampled some of the finest wines of the beautiful wineries of the region, an eternal harvest was being reaped at nearby Nelson Park and in schools and prisons.

As I stood among the counselors intensely engaged in conversation with those coming forward, I saw a counselor praying for a gang member. I saw a teenager with tears streaming down his face. There were people from many different cultures and religions present. A Muslim man said to a pastor, "Our faith is so somber. Only you Christians can put on something as joyful as this." There was a Sikh as well as fathers and solo mothers with their children. I saw some people leave during the altar call; perhaps it became too challenging. I observed a counselor speak to a group of young

Maori girls who had remained in the stands, somewhat subdued and smoking. He urged them to consider going forward to let Jesus fill the emptiness and loneliness of their lives. God was not only moving among those who had gone forward but also among the onlookers in the stands.

Into the Prison

"Inasmuch as you did it to one of the least of these, my brethren, you did it to me." Matthew 25:40

In the daytime, performing teams also had opportunity to visit prisons. Two vanloads of TX members returned to the Riverbend campsite near Hastings, where they were staying during their time in Hawkes Bay. They had been to the rural Hawkes Bay Regional prison, approximately eight kilometers south of Hastings. Ray Totorewa from Island Breeze had accompanied them.

"How did you get on?" I asked, as they joined us in the dining room. Rick, from Canada, Jason Hotere, and Ray were all grinning and eager to share their story.

"When we entered the grassy courtyard of the Maori Focus Unit, which was surrounded by the prisoners' cells, I was awestruck," Ray said. "I knew we had to be real to get through to these guys."

"About fifty prisoners, with their shirts off, performed the most ferocious *haka* I have ever seen!" Rick said. "Their earnest, spine-chilling, thigh-slapping, chest-hitting *haka* was not just a cultural display. This was the real thing! It made my hair stand on end! Some of them looked pretty mean, with their faces heavily tattooed."

"It was amazing to see their expressions change," Ray said. "At first they were aggressive and sat back with their arms folded.

As the TX guys bent bars, the prisoners soon got involved. They wanted to do it too."

"When I did the iron grip, clasping my hands," Jason said, "those big fellas really pulled hard!"

Rick continued, "As those two teams of inmates formed a human tug-of-war and pulled on your arms, the others watched the grunting, pulling, and eventual collapse."

"Rick explained how we need to keep focused in life," Ray said, "and not allow other people and pressures to pull us away. That's when we started to get through to them. The courtyard grew very quiet after we tore up telephone books and explained that God could forgive any sin. After the show, one of the inmates asked if God could forgive murder."

"They liked the TX testimonies," Jason said. "These big, rough fellas looked and talked just like them."

"Jason hit the mark when he preached," Ray said. "His words struck their hearts, and when he challenged them, about eight to ten stood, asking us to pray for them."

"After the show they showed us their cells and opened their hearts to us," Ray said. "We realized how similar we were to these guys. They faced similar challenges to us, with concerns for their families and their future."

"Just before we left," Rick said, "they honored us by presenting several *haka* and songs. I thought they would never finish! What a contrast to their initial hostility!"

"You guys did a great job!" I said. "The teams have lined up about eight more prisons for you to visit. I think it is one of the most effective areas of outreach. I wish I could be there with you!"

It did not matter where the gospel was shared—whether in stadiums, halls, prisons, or schools. The repeated phenomenon of hundreds of mostly youth and children responding at altar calls continued to amaze us. While we did not presume that all those who responded were genuinely converted to a lifestyle of biblical Christianity, the crowds of young people surging forward night after night never failed to move me. I thought that this response represented a true hunger in the land for truth presented in a culturally relevant way.

One keen IWT advocate helped me understand what was going on in the hearts of those who responded to the presentations of the gospel. He reflected on his own conversion in 1959 at a Billy Graham meeting in New Zealand.

"I didn't even want to be there, because Christianity at that stage of the beginning of my teenage years was contrary to my lifestyle. I thought that God really had no place in my life. However, I was intrigued as Billy Graham outlined God's purpose for man, the result of living selfishly, and how, in His love, God the Father sent Jesus to die in my place. I became aware of a huge emptiness in my life, and when Billy Graham invited those who wanted to repent and come to Christ, I found myself moving forward among them. I did not understand it all at the time and never did receive follow-up counsel, but over the next two years I was increasingly drawn to the things of God and eventually decided to become a follower of Jesus."[2]

Christchurch housewife Dorothy Gibson articulated a similar process as she had also responded thirty-five years previously at a Billy Graham altar call. "My heart was thudding in my ribs in a strange, sudden way. I didn't want to go out there in front of my friends—I don't know to this day how it happened—but suddenly the rebellion inside of me broke down and SOMETHING got me up on my feet and I was walking slowly down toward the front.... I believe it was the Holy Spirit of God that surged through me that night and walked with me all the way to the cross of His Son, Jesus Christ."[3]

When truth is spoken, either in one-on-one situations or publicly proclaimed, the Holy Spirit backs it up; people come under conviction and come into the Kingdom of God.

After all, the church began with Peter, previously an unpredictable fisherman, preaching his first-ever sermon (Acts 2:1-39). On the day of Pentecost, Peter, filled with the power of the Holy Spirit, outlined the essentials of salvation. He gave understanding of what God was doing on that day of Pentecost and spoke of Jesus' life, death, and resurrection and our responsibility to repent, be baptized, and receive the gift of the Holy Spirit. Three thousand responded to the gospel on that day, and millions have continued to do so ever since, as the gospel is shared.

Throughout history, preaching the gospel has always been one of God's methods of winning people to Christ. It may seem foolish to man, but the word of God spoken through human flesh is one way God uses. In *The Message,* Eugene Petersen paraphrases well God's wisdom in using preaching as His primary method of spreading the gospel: "God in His wisdom took delight in using what the world considered dumb—preaching, of all things!—to bring those who trust Him into the way of salvation" (1 Corinthians 1:21).[4]

As the modern-day GX dancers and skaters, the TX strong men, and the Island Breeze cultural dancers demonstrated and told the story of the gospel, many continued to respond as the Holy Spirit drew them.

Counselors

Be ready to give a defense to everyone who asks you a reason for the hope that is in you, with meekness and fear. 1 Peter 3:15

As enquirers moved forward, trained counselors accompanied them. Armed with their *Real Life* New Testaments and other materials, they prayerfully positioned themselves near someone of the same gender and approximately the same age.

While we aimed for one-on-one counseling, it was often more like one to three or even six, due to the numbers coming forward.

Mary, a counselor in Marton, shared that on that night she was trying to talk to six boys, all the same age. Her advice was, "Have plenty of counselors, absolutely heaps, because it's very difficult to be interviewing all of them at once."

It was not always possible to match counselors and enquirers, although we encouraged the counselors to try to talk with someone of their own age and gender. There were also many incidents of just the right counselor at the right time. Jay Lucas answered our office telephone one morning to speak to a young man who wanted to get in touch with the person who had counseled him, as he had some questions to ask him. Jay personally knew the counselor and was able to connect them.

Counselors had to be flexible during the evening performances. Three teenagers, trained as counselors for Wellington, commencing the following week, decided to attend an Upper Hutt performance to see how everything worked. They started talking to three girls, all dressed in black, who did not respond to the altar call but had remained in the spectators area. After talking with the counselors from Wellington for about an hour, the girls felt ready to commit their lives to Christ. When they met together at McCafe the following week, the three new believers were so bubbling over with questions that one of the counselors had them pass a McDonald's cup as they wanted to speak to create some order in their sharing and questioning. The counselors also accompanied them to a Youth Alpha Course, held at a Baptist church. One of the counselors became so excited at seeing others respond to Christ that she remarked, "This is what I want to live for. This is what the life of a Christian is all about. It's to be involved in seeing people become Christians."

Another teenager, nervous about sharing his faith, asked the Lord to lead him to the right people. He bounded up to Jenny Mollison and me backstage as we were finalizing some details for the evening. "Hey, Jenny, guess what! It was so much better than I thought. I talked with some guys from my school. They wanted to know everything. I found myself able to explain some things God had shown me. We're going to get together next week. Thanks."

Going Deeper

Strengthening the Church

"Many of the counselors were so nervous on the first night of the campaign. For some, it was the first time that they had ever shared their faith. My favorite part was the second night. I loved seeing how they had stepped out in faith. God had given them just the right words and their faces were almost aglow with enthusiasm, as they would share stories from the night before. I felt my own faith being strengthened listening to their stories and imagining how even the church people would be different afterward. I think a big part of what IWT is about is not just bringing people to the Lord, but also strengthening the church."

Julie McLaughlin
IWT staff

Testimonies from Counselors

I am willing to do the hard yards

One woman who had been spending three to four hours weekly with a troubled friend who responded at an altar call said, "I am willing to follow through with her. I am willing to do the hard yards."

This is the assignment for me

One counselor recognized that the seventeen-year-old Mormon he was counseling was sincere in his questioning, but needed more understanding. He continued to meet with him after IWT for more in-depth Bible study. He said, "This was the assignment for me."

Her teacher

My daughter's best friend, Jenny, responded. Jenny was turning around, smiling at the counselor. It was her teacher from school.

Are you any good at kids?

A woman tugged on my arm and asked, "Are you any good at kids?" I loved children and was able to sit down and talk with a seven-year-old boy and his mother on the grass and take them through the tract. I had met them before at Boys' Brigade.

Not just the young

Joy, who was not a very outgoing person, asked the Lord to lead her to the right person to counsel. She turned around and saw a seventy-six-year-old woman she knew standing at the altar call. This woman had lost her husband eighteen months before and was feeling quite lost and bewildered, without hobbies or interests. A friend from the Baptist church brought her to the campaign. This was the first time she had made a commitment to Jesus Christ. Joy was keen to keep in fellowship with her after the campaign.

Sometimes facilitators or members of the performing teams or task forces would step into a counseling role. One IWT coordinator, who had worked diligently and with joy in preparation for the campaign, did not want to miss the action during the counseling sessions. He picked up one of the *Real Life* Bibles and stood behind a gentleman who said, "This message was for me." Later on, his eight-year-old daughter came up to him and then they were joined by his twelve-year-old daughter who had also made a commitment. Finally, a woman with the joy of someone just given a priceless treasure joined them all and said, "Jesus is the center of our family now."

Jesus was there

Tony, a twenty-one-year-old male, asked if he could take a photograph. Rober, an Egyptian member of TX, asked him if he was a Christian, and although he said that he was, Rober was not convinced he was telling the truth. So he asked him if they could pray together. Rober was impressed by the Lord with a picture of this young man trying to hang himself. Tony said, "Yes, that happened, but my mum and dad reached me before I could hang myself." Rober encouraged him—"Jesus was there and He wants to give you life and has a plan for your life. You are here today and you are supposed to give your life to Christ." Tony started to cry as the Holy Spirit touched him and he became a true believer.

It's Jesus who loves you

Tash, a NZ member of the GX dance team, was standing on the outskirts of a group of people who had responded to the altar call. One of the girls came up to Tash and asked, "Do you do healings?" Tash explained that God does healings and discovered that this girl's sister was deaf in one ear. She began praying for her. Tash discovered that this girl was not a Christian and had been in the bathroom during the message. As the bus was leaving, Tash gave her best rapid-fire gospel message and shared the love of Jesus with her before saying good-bye.

Even if it was just for one man

Island Breeze performed in a Samoan church for about fifty people on Saturday night. A gentleman over eighty years old came forward and stood by himself for a long time. He was so serious about what he was committing to. Rudy Valle said later, "Even if it was just for that one man, it would have been worth it."

Spare time at the beach

In some spare time at the beach, I noticed a Maori male in his thirties. He had dreadlocks, and a big black dog was with him. I prayed that he would come to the show. The show went well. I did some log lifts. At the altar call I talked to the Maori man we had seen at the beach that day. He has three children and is separated from their mother.

Satanist comes to Christ

A woman Satanist had come to IWT because she had heard it was a Christian event and wanted to mock. Every time she opened her mouth to laugh, she cried instead. Thomas Hansen noticed her in the crowd and went to her after the performance. She ripped her necklace off and threw it to the ground. She began to repent, confessing that she had killed people's cats and needed forgiveness. She said she needed new clothes, new friends, and to start going to church. As Thomas prayed, she felt free from the occult.

Even outside of their performing schedule, team members were ready to share their faith.

Daniel Kim, an outstanding break dancer of Korean heritage, was en route to enjoy the swimming pool during some down time. He encountered three young Maori girls who cursed at Daniel and his friend as they walked past. "We hate God and don't believe in Him."

Rather than walking on past them, Daniel said, "God still loves you. Have you ever felt the Presence of God? If I pray for you right now, I believe you will feel that God is real." Soon after his prayer, one girl ran away, calling him a witch. As he talked with the two other girls, Daniel felt the Lord show him that one was angry with God because of the way her father had treated her.

She looked down. Then, looking Daniel in the eyes, she asked, "How did you know that?"

Daniel replied, "God speaks to us and wants to speak to you, too." He went on to explain the whole gospel message and there at the park bench asked the girls if they were ready to respond to Jesus. They did and their countenance changed from being mean and angry to smiles.

On another occasion, while enjoying a free afternoon at a beach in Auckland, Daniel was standing near a dance party with loud music. He felt the Lord prompting him to not only break dance but share the gospel with these people. In the few moments that followed, he had to decide whether to listen to the fear of man or obey the prompting of the Lord. He began walking up and down and shouting so as to be heard above the loud music. At the end of his spontaneous mini-sermon, ten young people decided they wanted to follow Christ.

Thomas Hansen was able to combine his passion for BMX with his love for reaching out to young people. Often he and some GX members would visit skate parks and were soon surrounded by young skaters, who would then come to the evening events.

David Hall, a YWAMer from Auckland, traveled with the tour, distributing literature. One evening a Maori man, sporting full facial tattoo, purchased a book for his wife. David, obeying the prompting of the Holy Spirit, gave him a copy of *Gladys Aylward,* the story of a missionary to China who accomplished great things despite many obstacles. The Maori man felt so personally challenged by the book that he invited David to his home the following evening. Over a hot drink, he shared part of his life story: drugs, prisons, Maori cult, and eventually Jesus. But his walk with God had been inconsistent and he had too easily gone back to some of his old habits.

Not missing the opportunity, David told him that it was no accident that he had given him that book. "God has plans for your life," he said. "But you've got to make a total commitment. It's all or nothing. Remember all the obstacles Gladys Aylward went through? But she didn't let those things keep her from doing what God put in her heart."

After further discussion, the man recommitted his life to the Lord and to all that God wanted to do in and through him.

The following evening, he enjoyed the final IWT night in his town. He was wanting more books—this time he went home with Loren Cunningham's book *Is That Really You, God?*[5]

I praised God for the thousands of performers, preachers, facilitators, counselors, servers, ushers, and intercessors who, like David Hall, were willing at any time to respond in faith to the prompting of the Holy Spirit.

It Wasn't All Easy

All the teams over these first weeks had to battle elements of the weather as they faced patchy rain and drizzle during many of the performances, and problems with transport and the technical gear. Andy Thornton was still fine-tuning the logistics for transporting the teams and equipment to multiple venues. Three containers were stranded in Palmerston North in the middle of the night. Somehow Andy, who by this time appeared to have his cell phone permanently attached to his ear, managed to get them transported to Wanganui just in time for the setup the following day. After my back-breaking experience of helping to lift the skate ramps off the trucks and trailers, I had an even greater appreciation of the commitment of the ramp teams to long hours of setup.

In Hawera, rain began to fall as the GX evening began, and then cleared as two bright rainbows appeared. At the end of the altar call, the generator suddenly cut. The same night in Wanganui, the rain came down half an hour into Island Breeze's routine. The team hurriedly covered the gear, and again the generator failed. Amazingly, most of the crowd remained at Cook's Garden Stadium. Backstage local team members and performers were fervently praying. An hour later, with rain easing and the power returned, Island Breeze came back on stage and people responded to Christ.

The battles the tech crew and all the teams faced, while testing, only strengthened their resolve to press on for the opportunity of preaching the gospel in the nation at this time.

These difficulties were, however, only a preparation for some of the most intense battles we were to face as we headed toward our capital city, Wellington, and the surrounding regions.

Chapter Twelve

Lashed by the Storm

He who observes the wind will not sow, and he who regards the clouds will not reap.

Ecclesiastes 11:4

Added to the normal challenges of transport and logistical problems was one we did not anticipate in summer—atrocious weather conditions.

"Frank," I said, calling our Dutch-born Hutt Valley co-coordinator, Frank Eijgengraam. "Make sure those contingencies are ready. There's a deluge coming! Mark and I will be there tomorrow."

"It's okay, Dave," he said, "the Executives here are working overtime to change everything."

The threat of adverse weather conditions over the last three weeks had intensified as the worst weather conditions in one hundred years lashed the lower half of the North Island. *The New Zealand Herald* reported that "the South Island and lower North Island will be hit the hardest, with strong winds and up to 150 mm of rain."[1] As the tour headed for the eye of the storm, the weather problems we had encountered during the first three weeks of the tour increased, as did the spiritual intensity.

I was glad the prayer surge around the nation, backed now by international intercessors and the prayer furnace raging at the IHOP in Kansas City. The estimated thousands of prayer warriors continued to pray for each town the tour visited, leaders and families by name, salvation of individuals and families, and the powerful presentation of the gospel with signs following. The weather was also a major prayer focus. The ramifications of the atrocious weather conditions were many. Indoor venues needed to be secured in every location but were usually small and inadequate. Teams needed to work longer hours, performing multiple shows and the tech teams had to tear down and set up equipment in the worst possible conditions.

For both the ramp and tech crews, even a light day in normal summer working conditions consisted of at least twelve hours of hard work, often early in the morning or late at night. The extra workload imposed by changing venues and more frequent performances pushed the crew to the physical limit.

After five days of relentless rain, most of the crew was forced to wearing wet shoes and clothes. Justin, a slim, wiry young American, recalls that in Lower Hutt his team had to pack the ramp gear three times in one day, setting it up finally at Hutt Valley Recreation Ground.

Just Keep Going

Finally, at 2:30 AM, I fell into bed, totally exhausted. My body was aching due to exposure to so much rain. The wind was still raging, creating an eerie atmosphere outside. The knock at the door woke me from a fitful sleep. I groaned inwardly when I heard the leader of the tech crew, Mark Howie, outside. "Justin!" His voice was raised in an urgent whisper, so as not to wake the household in which we were staying. "We've gotta go, guys. The roof has blown off the stage at Hutt Valley Recreation Ground. Justin, can you come?"

In resignation, I rolled out of bed, donned my last pair of dry jeans, together with my still-wet socks and shoes, and reluctantly joined the crew heading to the stadium. Silence was our companion as we willed our exhausted bodies into action. I was pushed to the limit and prayed silently, groaning inwardly, for strength to carry on.

When we arrived at the stadium, concern was mounting among the leaders there. The black tarpaulin covering the stage and gear had torn, resembling an evil hand tossed in the 80kph winds. Carefully, I climbed the truss, conscious of the force of the wind. "You can do it, Justin, just keep going," I kept saying to myself. At times my passion for extreme sports and for sharing the love of Christ with youth kept me going. We finished packing the gear down at 6:00 AM and managed to get a few hours sleep before returning for setup again at 10:00 AM.

I had to be broken before God. There was no way I could carry on in my own strength.

Justin Watson

At the Walter Nash Stadium in the Hutt Valley, torrential rain came down during the meeting on the first night, flooding the streets outside. Some plywood used for the GX ramps was used to construct a makeshift path over the water to enable people to leave the building after the performance. Despite the conditions, approximately one hundred people responded to Christ. During the next evening, some young gang members responded to Christ, while others were fighting outside.

Bad weather was not the only thing thrown at the teams. In nearby Masterton, when Nate, a Rollerblading GX evangelist, started to preach, a group of teenagers yelled at him. Nate, undeterred, continued his message of hope and new life in Christ as they threw food at him. Amazingly, many young people poured forward to give their lives to Christ.

It takes a lot of courage

> *Masterton is a really tough crowd to perform in front of. What you do takes a lot of courage and it surely shows God's Spirit is with you all. I freaked out at how many peoples' lives you touched through your testimonies. Two of my children gave their lives to Jesus at the TX show. Thank you for what you are doing for youth here in New Zealand.*
>
> *Received through IWT e-mail*

Members of the Hutt Valley Executive Task Forces refused to let the weather, crowd upsets, long hours, and constantly changing plans rob them of the promised harvest. They spun into action arranging alternate venues, communicating changes of plans, and together making decisions with the IWT national leadership. It was a beautiful picture, in the midst of adversity, of leadership and parts of the whole body of Christ in this region working together for the sake of the gospel. I thought that Philippians 1:27 could well have been written of these leaders. "*Whatever happens, conduct yourselves in a manner worthy of the gospel.... Stand firm in one spirit and contend as one man for the faith of the gospel*" (NIV).

The only time the grounds did have to be closed because of the conditions, we sought the Lord, with the basement of the Hutt Valley Recreation Grounds becoming our makeshift altar. As the tech crew packed down yet again and the wind raged, the Lord continued to test and sort our hearts, just as He did in the story of the windstorm with His disciples—*"Why are you so fearful? How is it that you have no faith?"* (Mark 4:40). Lurking in the shadows of our own hearts we found again subtle areas of fear, anxiety, unbelief, and our archenemy, pride. How devious our own hearts can be as we are entrusted with proclaiming the greatness of God. While performing team members, facilitators, and task force members alike had stepped up to the challenge of proclaiming His love, we discovered again in the cauldron of extreme pressure, flaws and dross in our own character that needed cleansing through repentance and confession.

Despite our shortcomings, our response to the storms had to be faith-filled confidence and rest in God. While we needed to examine our own hearts, we could then arise with renewed faith, boldness, and courage. Mounting a counter-offense, we called on all those involved in this campaign to fast and pray.

Mark challenged everyone again with the main focus of why we were in New Zealand: "This is not just about people coming to Christ. This battle is about the destiny of New Zealand!"

As far as the cancelled performance, the Executive Task Force opted for a redemptive approach, scheduling four extra performances. There was no stopping them!

Emergency Prayer Request

This is a time to contend and war in the spirit. In war terminology the enemy has mounted a counteroffensive.

I'm asking everyone connected to this outreach to step up their prayer and spiritual warfare. This is a critical time concerning God's plan for the outpouring in New Zealand.

The National Director for IWT, Dave Cole, and I are asking our team to fast and pray until the situation turns around. Others around the world may join us as they feel prompted by the Lord.

Let's watch together the Lord do mighty things in Wellington!

Mark Anderson

Wellington

In our capital city, Wellington, storms continued to rage with fury as the IWT volunteers waged their own battles. Teams of intercessors had been intensely praying for the city during the buildup to the campaign. Pastors and leaders gathered in humility to seek the Lord for their city. Numerous prayer requests were sent all over the world via e-mail during the next two days as the teams persevered through unabating weather conditions. Mel Gibson's movie *The Passion of the Christ,* showing the death and resurrection of Jesus in a powerful way, was released in New Zealand at the same time that the tour was in Wellington. I realized that God was orchestrating events in ways we never could have planned. Discussions about the film made headline news and filled talk-back radio shows, right alongside some of the shake-ups in government occurring that week. Intercessors everywhere had more than enough fuel to keep the prayer furnaces burning!

Prayer Request

February 17, 1:00 PM

It's raining again in the Wellington area. Officially now, this is the wettest summer on record, but we are determined to continue conducting our evangelistic campaigns.

Please pray for the following:

- That the rain would cease and the ground would dry. While this is a continuing prayer request, we don't want to be distracted from praying for the greater need for the growing move of God in New Zealand.
- The teams and staff working in New Zealand. The complications caused by the weather have created tremendous challenges for all of our workers. They are all working long hours.
- Favor with the media. The venue changes caused by the rain need to be re-advertised.
- Financial release. Again the complications due to the weather have increased our budget and we still need to raise an additional $300,000 for our overall costs in the next few weeks.
- Wisdom for leadership and staff. Decisions are being made minute by minute and we need to make the right ones.

Thank you for your prayer covering,

Mark Anderson
IWT International Director

The purpose-built stage had been damaged the previous week in the storm, and the stage from the Hutt Valley Recreation Grounds could not be moved to Basin Reserve in Wellington because of the waterlogged conditions of that ground. At 3:00 PM Wednesday, I called Oceania Productions to see if the stage used in Masterton could be relocated to Wellington by 7:00 AM the following day. The crew should have left this stage standing, but somehow they had managed to pack it down, so it was available for use. However, it would cost an additional $25,000 to hire and transport the stage from Masterton to Wellington. Since the main road had been damaged in the floods, the truck carrying the stage would need to negotiate a long detour.

At the Celebration Launch of IWT in Wellington that night, we felt that in the midst of our battle against the elements, God was requiring us to align ourselves with the Word of God and each other on a deeper level. We felt that we were to live in a new measure of the fear of the Lord, as the writer exhorted the Hebrew Christians: "*Therefore, since we are receiving a kingdom which cannot be shaken, let us have grace, by which we may serve God acceptably with reverence and godly fear. For our God is a consuming fire*" (Hebrews 12:28-29). Those present at the celebration launch for IWT in Wellington knelt publicly before the Lord, confessing the sin in identificational repentance of the body of Christ and the nation.

With faith rising, the local community, not wanting to see the work of the last six months aborted, raised $23,000 for the hire of the stage. The stage left Masterton at 2:00 AM Thursday morning, arriving at Basin Reserve at 7:00 AM during the only glimpse of sunshine we had seen for many days. Because of the apparent improvement in weather conditions, the grounds people gave permission for the evening show to continue. The task force all rejoiced. However, I was a little apprehensive since the gathering black clouds and hurricane-force wind-warnings indicated even more horrendous conditions to come than we had experienced so far. I did not want to be swayed by the enthusiasm and commitment of the team and felt a great sense of responsibility toward all who had given so much.

"I believe we should carry on, Dave," said Mark. "We have a history in IWT of performing where there are unusual and unseasonable weather patterns. I believe the weather pattern is a graphic picture of what is happening in a spiritual sense in this nation, as we intensify our efforts for the eternal destiny of the people of this nation."

While I was inclined to agree with him, I still felt a sense of responsibility toward the team. As I prayed, however, I did feel the peace of God in my heart, which I had come to trust as a good referee in difficult situations.

Mark continued, with determination forged through many battles. "In the book of Acts we read where Peter and John were told not to preach, but the apostles prayed and believed God for greater boldness and preached even more. This should be our response today." (See Acts 4:13-33.)

"Let's go for it and see God come through," I responded.

The atmosphere was electric as prayer intensified backstage before TX was due to begin. Finally, with the stage erected to only one-third of its normal height, TX boldly came on stage, without using usual video projection gear, and against a background of thunder, lightning, and driving horizontal rain. The crowd cheered loudly as the team performed feats of strength. Jason and the rest of the team cut out a lot of humor and went straight to the heart of the gospel message. Despite the conditions, people again surged forward to respond to Christ's claims on their lives. I felt that the adverse weather conditions helped people in weighing their decision to follow Christ—it made them seriously count the cost. Even to come out in such conditions was a great act of faith!

A pastor attends TX night at Basin Reserve

> *"I have never been in such an intense prayer meeting as that held at Basin Reserve before the IWT performance. Everyone was crying out to God as though his or her life depended on it. Some performing team members from other nations had puffed eyes through weeping over the sins of this nation. As I surveyed the smaller-than-expected crowd of around eight hundred, I thought they were most likely the diehard Christians. They cheered loudly as TX International performed feats of strength in the midst of terrible conditions. Even though the performance and preaching were short, when the altar call was given, a hush came as the weather quieted down. I could not believe it when over a hundred people streamed forward to find refuge in Christ, a true shelter from the storm."*

Further urgent prayer requests went out on the afternoon of the final day of the tour in Wellington, as storm-force winds up to 110 kilometers per hour whipped the stage and stadium.

One youth group from Wellington felt that the Lord showed them that the weather would clear by 6:30 PM, just in time for the GX performance. Clad in jeans and jackets, they walked seven times around the Basin Reserve Stadium, praying accordingly. What a faith builder and lasting effect for these thirteen- to fifteen-year-olds as the weather above Basin Reserve began to calm at exactly 6:30 PM!

As the winds began to die down two hours before start time, the weary tech crew, GX team members, and task force members alike were ecstatic. GX gave a passionate presentation of the gospel to the largest crowd that had ventured out over the last two weeks, and subsequently the largest response at the altar call.

> ### *Marlin's Diary*
>
> ***It was a great night. There is something powerful about defying the odds and going ahead with a show. It is like defying the enemy. God always works powerfully in these times. We had real victory in Jesus.*[2]**

Testimonies

Breaking walls of sin

"As we saw those men break walls of bricks, we knew walls of sin were breaking down."

I'll get back on track

"It was overwhelming. Everyone was getting up and I thought, 'I've been getting into a lot of trouble. I should go up and get back on track.' I had been getting into drugs, alcohol, and hanging out with the wrong crowd."

From the brink of suicide

"I tried to commit suicide about three weeks ago. When I heard Tatiana's testimony [video roll-in], it spoke to me because I'd felt the same as her. I feel so lucky that my friend invited me here tonight. God loves me. The void in my heart has gone. I want to tell other people."

You have to act

"When you hear a message like the one tonight, it's something you have to act on."

I wanted relationship with the Lord

"I just wanted that relationship with the Lord. I didn't want to miss out. At least I know where I am with the Lord."

Second chance

"I'm happy that I've made the right choice. I missed the opportunity yesterday and did not want to miss it again. So in the end I went up, and I'm very, very happy."

I haven't been living for Him

"I thought I should re-commit myself to God, as I haven't been living for Him. I felt warmth come through my body and I just up and walked to the front."

I now have a better understanding

One Island church leader said, "I now have a better understanding of who Jesus is."

Christianity is so cool

A man from a Baptist church brought some kids along to the IWT evenings. The children now thought Christianity was "cool." He felt his kids had a greater openness to spiritual things from their parents because of exposure to IWT.

I just wanted to be with Jesus

"I just wanted to be with Jesus, to give my life to Him. To know where I am going."

Jay was nearly bursting with elation, as his eyes welled with tears, when he heard all that was happening in the stadium and sent a phone text to all. "Way to go, team! Keep up the good work. Our struggles are cashing in with the freedom of transformed lives! Praise Him!"

We believed that these two weeks in the Wellington and Lower Hutt Regions won great victory for those who persevered under horrendous conditions to see the gospel of Jesus Christ proclaimed. All the teams proved themselves worthy of our prayer, support, and encouragement as they expended themselves to see breakthroughs in the spirit realm in this nation. None of us who were involved in those two weeks would ever forget it.

"Well, Mark," I said, "things might settle down now for the rest of the tour. It can't get much more intense than this!" Little did I know that our personal adventure was only just beginning.

Chapter Thirteen

Breakthrough in Tauranga

Behold, how good and how pleasant it is for brethren to dwell together in unity!… For there the Lord commands the blessing—life forevermore.

Psalm 133:1, 4

March 1, 2004

As we officially entered autumn, we geared up for two of our most intense weeks of the tour. Teams divided for a total of twenty-seven performances in the first South Island venture and in the Bay of Plenty and Waikato regions in the North Island.

Sue and I and our three younger children joined the tour in Tauranga in the Bay of Plenty. It was good to see our son Josh and the team.

"How's it going, Josh?" I asked when I called him. Josh was at the Bay Park Stadium.

"Great!" he said. "Everyone is buzzing here with preparations."

I could hear the TX members praying in the background.

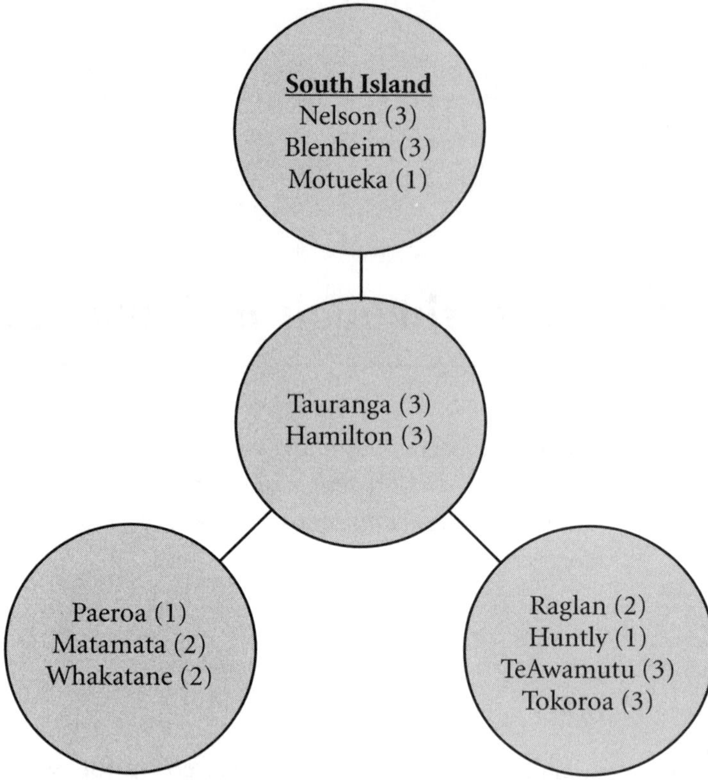

Josh continued. "It's incredible how the people of Tauranga have got behind this! People from over forty churches are coming tonight. One youth group already had ten teenagers become believers this week."

"Really?" I asked.

"Yeah. The youth leader began weeks ago to prepare the youth for IWT. She went all out, encouraging them to come to youth nights as well as the performance evenings. They had such an amazing response that even the week before the tour came to town, they had ten new decisions for Christ. We're looking forward to these three nights!"

"Good, Josh. We'll catch up later."

There seemed to be an unidentifiable dimension in Tauranga, as though the weeks of intensive prayer and battles had begun to gain some ground. Even the weather began to settle down! It was not just the numbers of young people responding to the gospel, or the large crowds that came for the evening meetings, or even the excellent performances of the teams. In Tauranga I realized we had observed one of the key components to the success of the campaign in that city, or for any endeavor for God—unity.

I rejoiced as I remembered the initial struggles of forming an Executive Task Force and working through budget areas with them. I admired this team as it had picked up the challenges and worked through them. During the buildup to the tour, God had brought about an unusual level of unity among the pastors of the city.

In May 2003, Brian Hathaway, at that time the principal of the Bible College of New Zealand, had addressed a large group of believers attending a Taruanga combined church service on the topic *How Does God Do Mission?* His answer was simple—through unity. His challenge was provoking: "If God does mission this way, why don't we?"

Going Deeper
How Does God Do Mission?

The principle upon which God has worked to make it possible for the evangelization of nations is the principle of unity. The question we have to ask is, "Why on earth do we think we can do it differently?" In John 17: 23 Jesus prays, "May they be one as we are one that the world may believe that you have sent me."

If we were one, the world would believe who Jesus is!

We have tried many evangelistic approaches, tools, and methods over the years. God in His grace has blessed them to a measure. However, I believe that we have yet to try the greatest tool for evangelism and, as I understand it, the one tool that has guaranteed success—Christians working together.

We desperately need some trailblazers. Some Christian leaders of churches in a town or in a city who have the courage to say, "Enough of this madness. Let's work together; let's pool our resources. It's death to our egos, but we want this town to be genuinely impacted for Jesus."

Brian Hathaway
National Principal of the Bible College of New Zealand

His word was so provoking that the following day (a day off for most of the pastors), a group from the Tauranga Ministers Association met together to discuss this important issue of unity and how they could apply it in the city. Six months later, on November 29, 2003, before a group of 750 believers, sixty-nine church leaders signed a Covenant of Unity. This agreement, in essence, bound these men and women to base their lives on the Scriptures as their Supreme Rule of Faith and Duty, to believe in the truths expressed in the Nicene Creed, and to "uphold, affirm and support the ministers, churches and ministries that God has placed around us in the City of Tauranga." Within the city leaders, God had found a humble group of men and women who were prepared to work together. IWT gave one focus for that. Most of those who became involved in IWT were already busy people. Yet among them were those who stepped forward and said, "Let's pool our resources. We want to impact Tauranga for Jesus."

I had witnessed pastors and leaders hold to their Covenant of Unity as we worked through issues in a spirit of humility and of honoring one another. The breakthrough in Tauranga had to result from far more than just the efforts of those who worked so hard on this project. It was the power of multiplication and blessing that came through unity.

So far during the tour I had seen the beauty of local believers rising up to do something together in their community that they could not do alone. In Hutt City I witnessed the extraordinary unity and perseverance of business, civic, and church leaders prevailing together for their city. In the South Island town of Blenheim, the counselors included the "One Church, Many Congregations" brochure with other discipleship materials. Christians in towns around the country showed a high level of unity in reaching out to their communities in the preparation phase. The barometer of prayer was increasing as prayer warriors from all streams united together. Task Force members from different towns commented, "Even if we don't hold the tour, the greater levels of unity have been well worth it so far!"

In town after town I observed the potential dividing seam of the local church and the international mission arm of the church become a place of mutual strength as each part operated according to God's design. I believe that God's intention has always been for the different streams of the church to work alongside each other. Where the local church welcomed the mobile and international church, and where IWT honored the local church, great synergy occurred. Where that unity in commitment to evangelism and to one another was backed by fervent prayer, God moved in ways that went far beyond any of our meager efforts alone.

Going Deeper
One Church—Two Redemptive Structures

Many people say, "If only the local churches were fulfilling their God-given mandate of evangelism and missions, there would be no need for mission agencies and para-church organizations." I first realized that God had designed *two* unique structures to fulfill His redemptive mission in the earth through Ralph Winter's landmark address, "The Two Structures of God's Redemptive Mission."[1]

Since World War II there has been an explosion of para-church and missionary movements. We have witnessed the blessings that have come through the working together of local churches and missions. One only has to look at the fruits that have resulted from the Billy Graham Crusades, the ministries of Campus Crusade, Navigators, Youth For Christ, Youth With A Mission, World Vision, as well as numerous other ministries. The potential for misunderstanding and tension is always there for any who work in either a local church or mission structure. Yet this can be overcome through humility and walking together in understanding of the God-ordained role of each structure. If there has ever been a need for the two structures to work together in unity, it is now! May we have His kingdom at heart and fulfill the Great Commission together. For His name sake!

Hank Overeem

Towns and communities that pulled together with the greatest level of unity and prayer in the preparation phase saw the greatest harvest, established excellent follow-up networks, and held an ongoing commitment for evangelism in their community.

We had not set out on a unity campaign! But as local believers in all spheres aligned themselves to Christ's command to preach the gospel, an increased functional unity within the body of Christ was the inevitable result. I believe it is one of the main reasons for the success of the campaign in those towns. Just as a net is joined and knotted to catch and hold fish, so the spiritual nets we cast to see people brought into the kingdom of God must be tied and knotted through relationships and prayer.

During the daytime, Mark and I met with other leaders on the ground floor of a seaside apartment block near Mount Maunganui. Loren Cunningham, some business leaders, and a representative from the International House of Prayer (IHOP) in Kansas City had also come for a firsthand view of what was going on in New Zealand.

On the last day of our meetings in Tauranga, Jay Lucas led us in worship, followed by intense prayer for New Zealand. Every prayer meeting I had attended recently seemed to be more intense than the last! In my own heart a shift was happening, right in the midst of the frontline battle in the tour. Although I was thrilled at the numbers of people being touched through the campaign, I was becoming more concerned with the importance of building on what God had begun in many communities so far. We quickly turned to this topic in our meeting.

John Banks, a businessman and the chairman of the Hutt Valley Task Force, was still glowing with reports of the tour in Hutt Valley. "As the performing teams left the rain-drenched Recreation Grounds," he said, "I turned to our co-coordinator, Frank Eijgengraam, and asked him, 'What about the ninety percent who were not here for IWT? How are we going to impact them with the gospel message?'"

"Good question," Mark said, chairing the meeting. Mark had already been to some post-tour celebrations in different communities. "In the few towns I have visited after the tour," he said, "people are asking, 'What's next?' That's because there is a next!"

John Banks carried on, "Some members of the Executive Task Force in the Hutt Valley, including Frank Eijgengraam, are continuing to meet together to seek God's strategy to impact the area. We plan to build on the prayer and relational networks that were strengthened through IWT."

"That is exactly what IWT was intended to do," I said. "To establish a beachhead, to take the work of God forward in each community."

"Not only in the local community," Mark said, always seeing the big picture. "I believe New Zealand is a launching place to impact other places, especially Australia, the Pacific, and Asia."

Rhonda Hughey, the IHOP representative, spoke up. "Central to the ongoing work of the body of Christ is a prayer furnace. We must establish a foundation of worship, intimacy with God, and corporate prayer for any work to impact a city or a nation."

Rhonda had just articulated what for me was the most important lesson so far in IWT. The increase in prayer around the nation and the dimension added through IHOP brought our efforts in evangelism to a new level. I was finding more and more that despite the many people coming to faith in Christ, my greatest longing was to experience more of the presence of God. I agreed wholeheartedly with her.

For the next three hours, our discussion revolved around these three themes, of ongoing outreach into the community, citywide expressions of worship and intercession, and mission endeavor. Ideas flowed back and forth over the next three hours as we discussed the "what's next" question. We needed to establish, both in local communities and overseas, centers that would serve the ongoing work of the harvest.

Until that afternoon I had presumed that my family would return to Singapore soon after our part in the tour was over.

What if we, like Frank Eijgenraam in the Hutt Valley, continued to serve the ongoing work of God in the nation? Where would we base ourselves?

Returning to our spacious apartment, Sue and I again considered our future.

"Do you think God is asking us to remain in New Zealand?" Sue asked.

"I'm not sure," I replied. "We've always thought that IWT was a catalyst to further the work of God in the nation. It would be easy for us to complete the tour and then head straight back to Asia once our role is over."

"What if our role involves more than we initially thought?" Sue asked.

Although there were four weeks before the completion of the tour, I could see wisdom in remaining in New Zealand. I wanted to see continued citywide expressions of the body of Christ, both in sustained prayer and worship and in ongoing efforts to influence communities and nations for Christ. Was the Lord alerting us to an ongoing assignment in New Zealand? One that could perhaps have a greater effect in Asia than our going there? Where would we live if we did remain in New Zealand?

I knelt with Sue with my elbows on the cane-backed, blue-cushioned apartment sofa.

"Lord," I prayed, "You lead us in our next steps." I was soon asleep on my knees.

That evening in Tauranga, the GX performance was outstanding. Over ten thousand young people streamed into the stadium. Loren Cunningham and other leaders from our daytime meetings joined the backstage prayer before the performance. When asked what effect he thought IWT was having on the nation, Loren replied, "I think it is powerful, because it enters into the world that young people are living in, like Jesus when He came and entered into the world we live in. It's the Incarnation of the gospel. The sports people are identifying with kids that are looking up to sports or are involved in it. The cultural show last night was entering into the culture that people are living in. They connected with it."

Everything seemed to have come to a new level, literally, when one of Australia's foremost FMX riders performed phenomenal stunt jumps up ramps, flying high over the stage as the crowd roared for more. Natasha Johnson, a Tauranga-born GX dancer, preached her first-ever short sermon and, at the close of the evening, with an authority born of a life transformed by the living Christ, called those many girls who had felt hurt and let down in relationships to respond to Christ.

I watched a sea of youth surge forward in response.

Tauranga Testimonies

I want to change my way of life

"I have had a pretty screwed up life and I want to change it. The stories some of the guys told were similar to my story. I've been a little sadistic lately, with the love of cutting myself. I am getting help. Now I am slowly changing, and committing my life to Christ is going to be the best thing I could do. Although I have been going to church for the last couple of weeks, I haven't been really sure about it. Now I am really sure."

My heart was pounding

A young woman who had been unsure of her standing with God and in her own words, "juggling around," said, "Hearing what the team members were saying just really got to me. I could feel my heart pounding and I thought,

'I have to go up.' Everything will be clearer now, just to know that God is there."

My Bestie and her cousins

"My Bestie and her two cousins gave their lives to Jesus and I feel great 'cause I took them there."

I had a fantastic time

"I had a fantastic time. The dancers were great and the lights and stunts were fantastic! The best part of it was that I walked away from the show knowing I have given my life to Jesus."

Thirteen-year-old girl

I'm not into that sort of thing

On the way home from the GX night, a young man picked up a sixteen-year-old hitchhiker. When asked if he had responded at the GX night, the hitchhiker said, "No, I'm not into that sort of thing." The driver shared his testimony with him and more of the gospel. By the time they arrived at his house, he invited Jesus to be the Lord of his life.

From out of town

I counseled a young Samoan man who had come to Tauranga from Auckland for a volleyball tournament. The coach had brought the whole team along to Bay Park Stadium. After the tournament, as part of the follow-up, I was able to connect these young men with a youth pastor in Auckland. I also called the coach of the volleyball team to thank her for bringing the team to Impact World Tour. I found that although she was not a Christian, she acknowledged that it was a special night and that all the guys got a lot out of it.

Tauranga Counselor

In the Middle of the Night

I was still reliving the GX evening as I drove my family home.

"Dad, my ear hurts!" The voice of our eleven-year-old daughter, Alana, from the back seat of our car brought me back to reality.

"It's really sore, Dad," she repeated, holding her ear, when we arrived back at our apartment. Sue and I prayed for her, and then Sue, always pragmatic, said, "I think I had better take her to the doctor, Dave. You know the trouble our children have had with earaches over the years."

You take her, Dave, I thought I heard the Lord instruct me.

"I'll take her, Sue. You get some rest." Although it was 11:30 PM, I called Josh, who was still meeting with the Executive Task Force after the final campaign night, handling all the logistics.

"Baycare Medical Services, Tenth Avenue, Tauranga," he instructed. "There's an all-night clinic there."

I hope we are not there all night, I thought. "Thanks, Josh."

I walked up the steps to the emergency medical center and pressed the doorbell.

A tall, sandy-haired doctor was on duty that night. He introduced himself, ushering us into a consulting room.

"It could have been the sound system at Bay Park Stadium tonight," I offered, by way of explanation for Alana's sore ear.

Even my ears were still pounding with the reverberation of the maximum volume and beat the GX team pumped out.

"My wife and children were there also!" exclaimed the doctor. "I see you are from out of town. What brings you to Tauranga?"

I explained that as the National Director of IWT, I was visiting Tauranga both for the campaigns and for the concurrent daytime meetings. He looked sharply at me but proceeded to examine Alana.

Once he had diagnosed Alana's ear and prescribed some medicine, we continued to talk while Alana rested. He described how the Lord had appointed him as an intercessor in the city, and during the last ten years, he had been faithfully interceding during the night shifts when there were fewer patients to attend to. He often fasted for the city.

"In fact," he said, "moments before you knocked on the door, I had just eaten a hot cross bun, breaking a forty-day fast for the city, for IWT, and for some other areas I was interceding for. I sensed there had been a breakthrough."

The familiar text alert on my mobile phone informed me that the Executive Task Force had just completed compiling the outcome for the Tauranga campaign. "Well," I said, "as you have been praying and fasting in secret, I think it is right that you are the first in the city to know the total number of people who responded at altar calls."

I do not think you could have given a better reward to a man like this committed intercessor.

"So," he asked once he had absorbed this, "where to from here?"

We were not the only ones asking that question!

> **Phone Text Message:**
>
> ***Awesome night in Tauranga. Total response for 3 nights: 645 first time, 361 rededications, 152 other needs. Total 1,158.***

"Well," I began, sensing a great depth and heart of humility in this eager doctor, "we were discussing this afternoon the importance of building on what has begun through IWT. We desire to see ongoing corporate expressions of the local body of Christ, undergirded by sustained prayer and worship. We also want to see continued outreach impact the local community and a center for serving the campaigns in the Pacific and Asia regions." Although I could not outline then the extent of the vision that was enfolding before us, I sensed a strong presence of the Spirit of God in the emergency clinic.

The doctor appeared intrigued and was listening intently. "Where would you see this being established?" he asked.

"At this stage, Tauranga seems the most likely. We don't have any definite plans at this stage." I was surprised at how animated this doctor was becoming.

"This is amazing!" he said.

He then explained how he, together with others in Tauranga, had a similar vision for a training center that would equip young Christian leaders in different areas of service, both in New Zealand and in other nations. "Critical to this training center," he emphasized, "is the worshiping, praying heart of every believer.

"That was the other part of the fast I have just completed," he said. "In fact, I sensed a breakthrough today as I had just completed this fortieth day of prayer and fasting. That's why I was enjoying a hot cross bun before you arrived."

While he laughed heartily, I was aware that through our daughter's earache, God had brought us together in the middle of the night and that we had the same heart and ongoing vision. This had to be more than a coincidence, especially after our discussion and prayer that afternoon.

It always amazed me how God would show up in unexpected ways as we responded in faith toward Him. *Even if our faith is weak.* I smiled as I remembered falling asleep while praying.

Sue's concerned voice on my mobile alerted me to the fact that it was now after 1:00 AM. "Don't worry. We'll be home soon. I believe I have just had a divine appointment in the emergency clinic. It could be a signpost for our next step."

I looked at our daughter, who had nearly fallen asleep. "I need to take Alana home," I said to the doctor. "Perhaps we could meet together after the tour."

He wholeheartedly agreed.

Chapter Fourteen (a)

Let the Children Come

"Let the little children come to Me, and do not forbid them; for of such is the kingdom of heaven."

Matthew 19:14

"Where's Deborah?" Sue was frantically looking for our five-year-old daughter amidst the movement of the crowd as they came forward in Matamata after the TX altar call. Since Matamata was less than a two-hour drive south of Auckland, our children had accompanied us to the TX evening. I walked around the back of the crowd, peering in between enquirers and counselors, trying to find Deborah. Finally, Jenny, who was helping to oversee operations from the stage, signaled to me.

Standing right at the front of the stage, her crop of red hair bobbing up and down as she nodded her head intently in agreement with her counselor, was Deborah. She was responding publicly to her commitment to want to follow Jesus, which she had made with Sue and me years before. Relieved, I stood quietly behind the pair and talked briefly with the young counselor.

Deborah was one of thousands of children who responded at altar calls around the country. Some of them rushed forward, and as in Deborah's case, certainly not because of any peer or parental pressure! Many appeared genuine in their response and reflected the openness of children to the gospel.

When Michael and Pensy Lo-Schuemperli moved to Hamilton in October 2003 for some more on-site preparation for IWT, Pensy willingly took charge of the preparation for children's clubs. "The most important part of children's work is to show the heart of God for the children," she said, "coupled with a strategy to reach the whole city." With this in mind, Pensy enlisted helpers from around the city to discover, first, what was already operating, then what needs there were, and then what could eventually be put in place.

"You have to reach kids after school in their own environment," she said.

In one suburb of Hamilton, a children's club with twenty-five children started six weeks before the campaign. Some of these children invited parents and other children to the evening performances.

One Samoan church in Hamilton was slow to come on board in the preparation stage of IWT, but eight children committed their lives to Christ at the campaign. One woman called the IWT office and asked for help in discipling the children. This church and others in the region became involved after the campaign in the follow-up work.

Going Deeper

Keys to Establishing Successful Children's Clubs

Prayer for the children.

Friendship and partnerships in the city. Networks are built more on friendship and prayer than structure.

> *Love for the children.* Children respond to love rather than programs. We must show God's heart, His compassion, and prayer. Most of the children responding at IWT have never been to church.
>
> *Pensy Lo-Schuemperli*

One Anglican Church in Hamilton arranged for ninety-one children to attend IWT. Older people from the church baked cookies and many prayed. Eighty-five of the children responded. After the tour, thirty-eight children's clubs were established in Hamilton. Most were led by mothers, grandmothers, and teenagers. These were the willing volunteers who had a heart to reach out to children. It was certainly not about status, salary, or position but about having a heart and starting! I felt that these children's clubs were essential in follow-up.

The eleven-to-fourteen-year-old age group is often an age where children are pulled away from church involvement. Pensy found that eleven churches were already actively pursuing this age group. They met together for encouragement and prayer and to share resources. One week before the tour came to Hamilton, twenty-one clubs were ready for this age group across the city.

"Phew!" Pensy said after the tour. "I have never worked so hard in all my life!" I had observed Pensy at work in Auckland, overseeing Bible in Schools programs and starting children's clubs, so I knew that was saying something!

Testimonies

Not disruptive

> *"One boy in my class was particularly disruptive. For two weeks after IWT, he has been different. He was not mocking, not disruptive, but thoughtful and asking*

questions. He asked me if I had gone to IWT. He said he had and went up to the front to get a Bible. It is so encouraging to see such a change in him."

A child shall lead them

One girl, who used to come to our church before her mother was killed in a car accident, was not able to come to IWT but sat on the back porch and listened. Her father later brought her and her younger sister back to church on Sunday.

Others see problems

"Eight-year-old Emily came to my Bible in Schools class weekly. Since she lived near us, I was conscious of some of the details of her home life, which included various men moving in and out and her mother's coping with a severely handicapped older child. Frequent episodes of domestic violence occurred. When we invited Emily to come to IWT, she gladly responded to the altar call, and her green New Testament became one of her prized possessions. Others saw only problems in her life. Jesus sees the potential."

It felt good

Dear Impact World Tour,

Thank you for putting on the show for us.... I liked TX and GX. It felt good giving my life to God. Can you come next year? I would like to hear from you again.

Love from,
James

It was a good speech

Dear Impact World Tour,

...I really liked the guy that was talking about his life in Holland, it was a good speech. It was the thing that made me go up and give my heart to the Lord.

Thank you.

Love from Kimberley

My nine-year-old

"My nine-year-old son responded on the first night and got the TX guys to pray for him the second night. He has read the whole gospel and shared with some of his friends, who laughed at him, but he has held to his convictions."

Some Said "No"

I was grieved at the response of a few parents who did not want their children involved. One woman grabbed her children and walked out of the stadium when a video clip of Jesus on the cross appeared. She felt this was far too gruesome for children to see. Another parent wrote to the newspaper complaining that the children had been contacted by Christians after the event. Some felt IWT was too late in the evening for children.

But aside from these instances, there was very little negative response; the overwhelming response was very favorable.

Media

We were very much aware of the potential in the media for favor or for the damage that negative publicity could bring.

At our Silverstream meeting in December, our European coworkers told us how distorted front-page headlines had brought great damage to IWT in Sweden. "Christians Want to Kill Homosexuals!" ran the headline. This was a distortion of what the young GX preacher had actually said when referring to homosexuality from God's perspective. However, the damage was done, and one of our staff almost went to jail as a result.

Although there were occasional negative write-ups, I was pleased and somewhat relieved with the overall favor we found with the media and the accurate representations and true-life stories portrayed. The traveling media liaison team of three capable young women from the USA, England, and Australia were all kept busy using their skills in public relations and journalism to communicate with the media.

Kevin Stark and Jason Hotere from TX enjoyed their time on *The Holmes Show,* a highly rated evening current-affairs program at that time in New Zealand. During the broadcast they were able to perform a couple of mini-feats and give clear explanation of what they meant. I was standing next to an elderly woman at the Papakura campaign who had attended as a result of viewing *The Holmes Show*. "My!" she exclaimed, watching some of the TX International feats of strength. "Christianity has sure changed since I was at Sunday school!"

No, I thought, *the message is the same, just presented in a different way.*

Jason Hotere and a couple of GX leaders were also guests on the Sunday morning *What Now* program, which has the largest viewing audience among children in New Zealand.

Chapter Fourteen (b)

Shall I Not Be Concerned for that Great City?

"Should I not be concerned about that great city?"

Jonah 4:11 NIV

I could not have imagined a more picturesque setting for the commencement of sixteen campaign nights in the city of Auckland than Bastion Point. As the glowing red sky silhouetted the city's buildings in the east, and the backdrop of Rangitoto Island and the Waitemata Harbour faded underneath a calm, clear sky, the evening's program began on a somber note. Rocky Hawke, a key member of the Orakei Marae who had been instrumental in hosting IWT at Orakei Marae, had passed away that morning, having suffered a heart attack just days before. As the crowd observed a minute's silence in his memory, I noted the contrast in the atmosphere that evening compared to that of our arrival two days before. The tour had been welcomed with great joy and expectation in the traditional *powhiri,* hosted by the Ngati Whatua people at Orakei Marae. Now the gathered crowd was silent, somber.

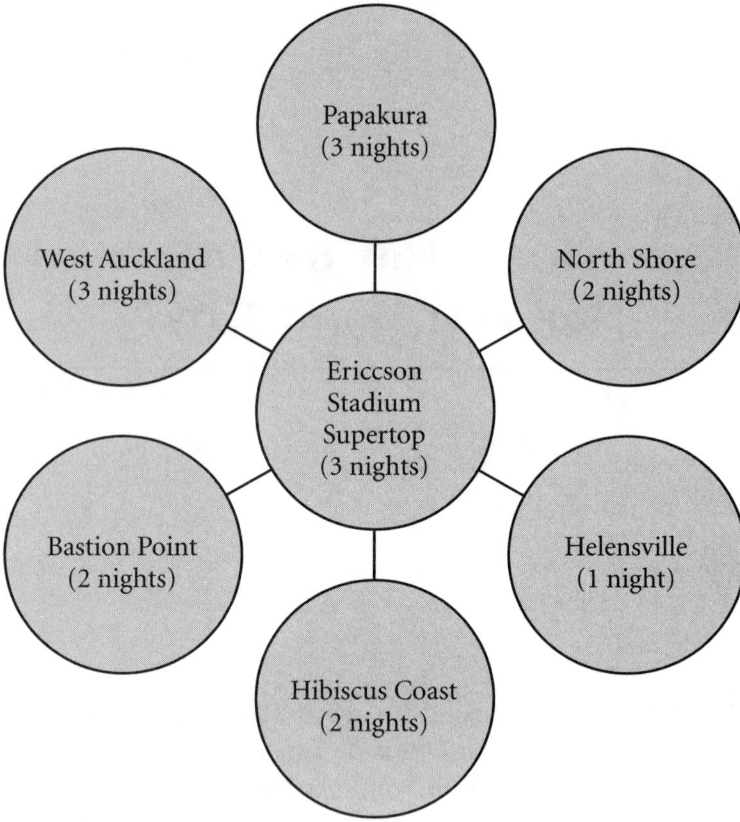

Rocky Hawke, together with his uncle, Bob, yearned to see Maori come to Christ and had expended themselves in preparation for IWT in this historic location. They were also working on a program to provide care for Maori inmates released from prison. Rocky's older brother, Joe, had worked hard in the previous generation to battle for the land rights of Maori. Now the battle continued for the souls of men.

A great attentiveness settled over the crowd as Island Breeze moved through their dance routines, highlighting the value and beauty of every culture, every person. The next day the TX team paid tribute to Rocky at Orakei Marae. "Thank you for coming," Bob said. "You are family now."

That evening as Jason finished preaching, he called his wife and two-year-old daughter on stage, together with all of the TX immediate family members. With this picture of *whanau* (family) on stage, many from the crowd came forward to discover their place in God's family. Among them was Jason's father.

Our own daughter Lisa surprised herself by thoroughly enjoying TX. "I didn't know Christianity could be so much fun!" she said. I sensed that, despite some of the pain of the last two years, Lisa's heart was beginning to respond afresh to the love of God.

As on the previous evening, I noted that people from a vast array of cultures were present. Among them were Maori, Pacific Island, European, Asian, and Middle Eastern people, representing the blend of cultures in Auckland's metropolis.

One of our staff later observed, "*Whanau* was the message heard loud and clear at Orakei Marae."

The two weeks in Auckland, New Zealand's largest city, saw no letup on the penetration and impact of the gospel as teams ministered in venues all over the city. Island Breeze and GX had opportunity to perform at *Pasifika,* a large Polynesian festival, which draws a crowd of approximately 170,000. Teams also visited key schools and prisons, having powerful times sharing with those present.

Auckland was like a sleeping giant, slow to awaken. The dynamics of city life meant there was a natural busyness to contend with. Auckland did not need more entertainment. To many, IWT was another event in another busy year, whereas in some smaller towns, this was the largest event that had ever been staged there. Many of the large metropolitan churches had full programs with effective outreach strategies and discipleship programs and, from their perspective, did not need another.

I could hardly believe that everything came together in time for the tour. Only six months before, the Auckland preparation was floundering, despite our best organizational attempts. Although Auckland had started well, with excellent fund-raising banquets and initial church support for the tour, it was now lagging far behind. No less than five IWT facilitators had to finish their commitment prematurely for a variety of personal reasons—visa problems, other commitments, family issues. Arrangements with venues secured months earlier fell through, and finances were lagging below target.

We had to decide whether to persevere or pull out.

As Jenny, Jay, and I met in the War Room, we earnestly sought the Lord. "We can't pull out now," Jay said. "Auckland is such an important city."

Jenny, always realistic, said, "Look. So many essential parts of the infrastructure aren't in place. It's impossible to do this without staff, venues, and resources."

In other aspects of the tour, including personnel, finances, and transport, I had seen the Lord unexpectedly turn things around as we trusted Him and persevered. "We have to stand firm in faith," I said. "There are some wonderful people of faith in Auckland who believe with us that many will turn to faith in Christ during IWT." Then I added, partly to reassure Jenny, "More than you realize."

Jenny smiled. "I'll trust you on that, Dave. It seems almost impossible at this stage."

"Without faith," I replied, "it *is* impossible."

A pivotal meeting occurred when I met with some of the Kaumatua, or spiritual elders, at Orakei Marae. Monte Ohia, who had led the Maori Gates Tour, joined me. Hugh Gollan, a businessman who had also been part of that tour and now played a key role in business aspects of the tour, was also with us. As we had done when we visited other marae, we shared the vision of IWT and sought the blessing of the elders. Bob

Hawke said it was in the 1960s that the last large-scale outreach had been hosted at Bastion Point. His brother Rocky, who had passed away the morning the tour commenced in Auckland, was also very keen on outreach in the community. In the next two months, these two men, together with those from Orakei Marae, drew together other Christians who had been praying for the surrounding area.

Only a few months before the Auckland campaign commenced, Fred Needham, a North Shore pastor, together with willing members from his church, Auckland Christian Assembly, took up the floundering North Shore organization. "With Mark 16:15 as our mandate," he said, "we need to get alongside any organization that will proclaim the gospel of Jesus Christ. If they are prepared to fulfill the mandate to go into all the world and preach the gospel to every creature, we are prepared to help them." I was astounded at how quickly they took action and helped to fill organizational positions to make the North Shore Campaign so successful. They hosted fifty to sixty TX International members on their property and worked tirelessly to set up discipleship and arrangement details.

Many Korean churches in the city were seriously praying about how to evangelize the youth. However, at the initial vision-casting meetings in Auckland, some leaders were shocked at the dance and other contemporary means of evangelism GX style. Jung Bee, our IWT facilitator, and the Korean Task Force persevered in relationship with the churches. Eventually the church leaders realized that just as Jesus left the glory of heaven to make the love of God known to us, we need to enter the world of our youth to reach them with the gospel.

The Koreans lived up to their reputation of fervent prayer as they prayed for the youth to be impacted by the tour. Business people gave generously. By the time the tour was launched in

January, over one thousand Korean Christians attended the Revive Auckland meetings at which Loren Cunningham spoke.

We gladly welcomed staff who came to assist us in the final stages of preparation. An American facilitator managed to rebuild trust with the leaders in West Auckland and assisted Helensville, outside of Auckland, to become involved at the last minute. Other staff, including Mark Anderson's daughter and son-in-law from the USA and a nine-member event management team from Townsville, Australia, provided much needed reinforcement for the final preparation stages in Auckland.

At the North Shore Events Centre, one Korean counselor was standing at the doors when they opened. She could not believe the rush of young people as they hustled to find a seat. Korean youth were among them. "I have never seen anything like this!" she said.

Later, as scores of young people stood at the altar, she counseled some of them. Afterward she stood with another Korean friend. They wept together. Through her tears she said, "I have never seen Jesus impact people like this. I love this." Through the course of the campaign she counseled over twenty people to faith in Christ.

Late in proceedings, our team managed to secure Ericsson Supertop, a huge tent-like structure behind the Ericsson Stadium, near our Auckland office. After the Island Breeze performance, John Komene, a prominent Maori elder and Dean of the Bible College of New Zealand, went backstage. He took Ray's and Shaneane's hands and profusely thanked them. "Seeing the gospel presented in this way to the Maori people is something I have dreamed of for many years. Thank you."

The following evening, I again felt like a spectator as all those involved with the setup, performance, and counseling went about their assigned tasks. Singers, dancers, rollerbladers gathered in huddles backstage when they were not performing, praying for the GX crowd. As Jesse Fellers and Tash Johnson gave a clear altar call, other GX performers prayed more intensely, some lying prostrate on the dirty stage. Pastors and ushers were shepherding the droves of young people coming forward. Life FM was broadcasting the performance live. Some from the radio-station van left the van, stunned at the hundreds of young people responding at the altar call.

Hugh Gollan kept me abreast of the difficulties of the Auckland preparation. I knew of some of the struggles he faced as a businessman with the uncertainties of venues and personnel, the difficulties of forming strong task forces and the disappointment in the Capital Campaign. With humility, he acknowledged that the logistics of IWT were not simply a matter of following a great business and finance plan. "Where God came through in Auckland," he said, "it was brilliant. Where we struggled without His leading, we were bound to fail. God was fulfilling His agenda, humbling us. We had to persevere to find His way."

I was grateful to Graeme Davison and the Pan-Auckland Committee and all the staff involved who did persevere. I was amazed at how all the preparations, in the end, came together. Even the budgets were met! Most of all, the lives of thousands of people were impacted with the gospel.

Auckland Testimonies

You go

Some of the organizing committee for IWT at Bastion Point came to relieve the young men serving as parking attendants. "You go and enjoy the show," they said. All of the young men responded to Christ.

A new youth group

For some weeks prior to IWT at Bastion Point, a Presbyterian church had organized a youth evening every Friday. Out of the fifteen youth from that group that attended IWT, fourteen of them responded at the altar call.

What's going on here?

"Some of my mates and I came up from Mission Bay when we saw the lights and concert. We said, 'What's going on here?' In the end, listening to Jason, we felt uplifted and so we came to the front. When we were asked if we wanted the beer back that we had brought, we said no."

A lesbian couple

A lesbian couple came forward to surrender their lives to Christ. They were counseled by two different counselors.

Not what we expected tonight!

Another young man came with a group of friends after hearing the music. Being up front at the altar call was definitely not what he expected that evening! "It's amazing!" he said, describing what had transpired. "Not what we expected tonight! You're just standing and thinking 'he's talking to me' and you forget everyone else is there."

It struck my heart

"I came because my friend invited me. For my age group it's really cool. It struck my heart; it's all new to me. It's the first time I've actually gone up and wanted to meet Him."

Time for a change

"I came forward to accept Jesus Christ as my Savior. I thought it was time for a change, to change my abuse of alcohol."

Two more for my friends

"I went forward after the GX night at North Shore Events Centre and someone gave me a Bible. I have been reading it and find it so helpful that I would like to get two more for my friends."

On the road

One couple was driving past Parrs Park in West Auckland and stopped to see what was going on. When they heard Nate, the young GX preacher, they came under deep conviction and repented of their backslidden state.

Chapter Fifteen

When Things Go Wrong

If anything goes wrong, take it to the cross.

We could not pretend that everything always went smoothly. Apart from battling the weather in the first half of the tour, there were numerous opportunities for things to go wrong—and they did!

In Tauranga, Jason strained every muscle in his body, attempting to pull a huge truck. No amount of enthusiastic cheering from the crowd helped him move it. When he finally gave up, someone heard the hiss of the air brakes, which had been left on! Surprisingly, this only endeared him to many in the crowd as it showed how human he was.

Although specifications were always given concerning materials used for the performances, occasionally oversights were made. In Auckland, a last-minute discovery of reinforced concrete blocks in place of the regular ones that TX use for breaking down walls, averted potential injury.

One of the feats of strength TX performed was to run through two two-by-four pieces of timber. "You'll need to be careful with that timber!" commented the man delivering the timber for the breakthrough run for TX in Nelson. "You could drive a truck over it!" Sure enough, that night, when Micah attempted to run through the timber as other TX members held the ends, Micah ended up in a pile on the floor and one of the men was knocked unconscious and went to the hospital. It was not the timber usually used.

Other TX members and some skateboarders and dancers from GX also suffered injuries. Long days and demanding schedules resulted in weariness for many. We had to take note of Paul's exhortation, *"Be sober, be vigilant; because your adversary the devil walks about like a roaring lion, seeking whom he may devour" (1 Peter 5:8).*

In all the battles we faced with the elements of nature, our own physical weaknesses, and sometimes carelessness, we could not always blame the devil when things went wrong. Organizing thousands of volunteers was bound to give occasion for relational, communication, or technical mix-ups. We had to be sure that we did not "give place to the devil" (Ephesians 4:27) but take responsibility when we fell short.

Issues of Spiritual Warfare vs. Battles of Life

I struggle with determining what the issues of warfare are and what the battles of life are. Several team members have been hurt—Franco sprained his ankle when we were wrestling; others have also been injured. One of the GX team had a freak car accident. Perhaps the enemy uses our weaknesses and vulnerability. We need to take spiritual warfare seriously. I need to make

> sure I don't leave weapons around that the enemy can use against me (unforgiveness, carelessness, poor relationships, etc.). We also can't blame everything on the devil. This will take the blame off where it belongs—on me. When we spiritualize everything, we don't accept responsibility for our own sin and shortcomings.
>
> *Marlin's diary*

How appropriate, I thought, was the exhortation at the Silver Stream pre-tour meeting that Frank Lauridsen, from Denmark, brought: "All through this, everything that goes wrong, take it to the cross." As local volunteers and team members did this and made a conscious effort to respond rightly despite bad weather, technical failure, character flaws, miscommunication, and all manner of things that could go wrong, and pressed in for the harvest of souls, hundreds of people responded every time the gospel was proclaimed. Like Paul, we learned that in our weakness Christ could show His power, *if* we responded to Him rightly.

As the performing teams headed south for two intense weeks in the South Island, nine weeks on the road had begun to take its toll. For many of the younger team members, friction had surfaced as they faced strenuous schedules along with the inevitable clashes that occur with pulling together multicultural teams. Bodies were tired and injured. The initial honeymoon phase of excitement and loving everybody was definitely over as teams faced reality checks in areas of immaturity and character flaws that surfaced under pressure.

The TX team daily gave opportunity for any relational difficulties to be worked out. Personal times of seeking God and group times of prayer, worship, and openness to one another became very important. "Don't let the sun go down on your anger," TX leader Kevin Stark would often exhort the team. Humility and forgiveness were expressed many times during the tour as team members had opportunity to humble themselves, to ask and receive forgiveness for acts of selfishness, pride, and immaturity. As Paul Subritzky, the leader of Promise Keepers New Zealand, observed, "It is a true demonstration of manliness to see big guys humbling themselves, crying, and praying together."

The whole team came to a deeper level of unity and repentance in Christchurch when Dan Baker, an American pastor, traveled with the performing teams for the remainder of the South Island Tour. He strongly encouraged team members to live with purity of heart and brought correction and instruction where needed. "You talk too much," he directed one young man. This young performer, along with others from the team, was soon under conviction of the Holy Spirit.

TX went on stage that evening with a renewed understanding of their role of presenting Christ as a team, not just being on stage as individuals. Somehow, as they had responded to the Lord, pressed in, and shifted gears, there was a different feel as the strongmen gathered for prayer and communion before the evening performance.

At the end of the performance Kevin Stark asked the crowd, "Are you right with God?" before breaking another pile of bricks to demonstrate the breaking down of the wall of sin that separates us from the love of God. At the altar call, 947 people went forward, indicating that they were not.

For some team members, the waves of people pulsating into the aisles at Westpac Centre, Christchurch, remained as a memorial to the power of God working through the weakness of sanctified, imperfect human vessels. They, like Paul, could boast, "*We have this treasure in earthen vessels, that the excellence of the power may be of God and not of us*" *(2 Corinthians 4:7).*

As the GX team headed further south, these were arduous weeks also. "In the midst of the pressure-cooker experience," said Jesse Fellers, one of the GX leaders, "I had to ask myself and our team members, how do we respond? Do we respond with faith and love as the junk in our own lives comes out through pressure, or do we draw back? If we respond with love and blessing, God will touch areas of our own lives. If we fail to respond rightly, our hearts become hardened, offended, and bitter, and we can become distant from the youth the Lord has sent us to reach." In Timaru, with only two weeks remaining of the tour, Jesse strongly appealed to the GX team. "Let's give everything to the tour. Let's go the full 110 percent. We need to pour everything in and finish strong." There was quite a commotion during the GX night in Timaru, with fights, drunkenness, and members of the crowd yelling abuse. Jesse's own heart was touched with renewed desire to cooperate with God to see the Holy Spirit touching young people.

Press On

There are times when we will not feel like ministering, but it is during those times of weakness that God will come through with His strength. I cannot rely on my own strength. True ministry can only take place through the power of the Holy Spirit.

Marlin's diary

In Reefton, on the west coast of New Zealand, local organizers joined in the worship before the tour. Months later, they were still talking about the impact it had on them. In a small town, everybody knows everybody. One pastor's wife remarked, "I know some of those people responding at the altar and they have not been churchgoers!"

Busloads of people came from the nearby west coast towns of Greymouth, Hokitika, and Westport. For many on those people, Reefton became a "City of Light," as the welcome sign says at the entrance way to the town.

From the Ends of the Earth

I was glad that the southernmost city in the world, Invercargill, had eventually embraced IWT and worked hard in preparation. During the many times we prayed for this city, we sensed that part of the destiny of this Southland area was to send God's Word from "the ends of the earth" to the four corners of the earth. Southland Stadium filled to capacity for Island Breeze, and for the GX night, two to three hundred people were turned away from the second performance. Fighting broke out as some youth tried to break through the crowds to get in the doors.

Leaders from towns where IWT was not hosted did all they could to invite young people to the campaign nights. A busload of people came from the scenic, mountainous tourist town of Wanaka to the nearby town of Cromwell, while a policeman, together with other Christians, organized a busload of young people from the lakeside town of Te Anau to attend the evenings in Invercargill.

Youth Get a Big Dose of the World

From where I sit, the youth of today get a big dose of the world, 24/7, and it was good for our youth to see some Christians who were cool. In a small town like ours, many youth feel alienated from the Christian-stereotype culture.

If there were ever an event like this one, I would work like a madman to bring them to our town.

If we had some of your skaters and dancers in our little town, they could impact the youth immensely. Something special happens when dynamic role models are able to share a few minutes of their lives and earn the right to speak into the lives of youth. This was very much a seed-sowing exercise. I am sure that we are yet to see all the fruit from IWT, but we are praying for some key youth that responded in Invercargill. The next step is exciting.

Te Anau policeman

In the satellite towns of Alexander, Cromwell, and Oamaru, the wonderful spirit of unity and cooperation combined with faith and love resulted in many finding faith in Christ.

In a commitment to sharing the gospel with all, when Terry Kabala from Invercargill arranged for Jason and three other TX members to visit the small nearby town of Winton, they did so willingly and prayed for hours in undertaking this overnight trip. Over two hundred young people turned up to see the Big Men. One of them contacted Terry later, saying, in the language of youth, "Wow, what an awesome night!" Jason and the team left under darkness to join the rest of the team the following night in Alexandra, having felt that they had made a "sneak attack" and rejoicing again in the response of this small community.

At first glance, the unusual small tri-generational group that gathered at the top of Mount Cargill, overlooking the bleak, hilly city of Dunedin, had little in common. The IWT prayer coordinator, together with some local intercessors and leaders, had gathered to pray for the city. I had joined them, as did a Fijian pastor, an eighty-five-year-old intercessor known as Violet, and a few other interested people. During the next

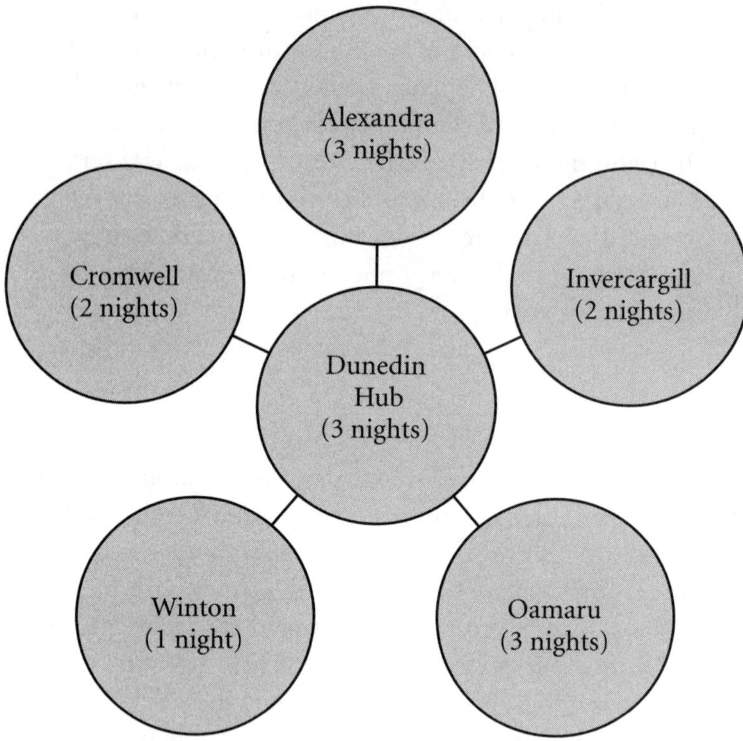

several hours, our hearts were together as we interceded for the city. Violet, who had been consistently praying for Dunedin for over forty years, saw IWT as part of an answer to her many prayers. We invited this fiery elderly woman to join the TX prayer and worship before the evening performance. Part of our prayers on Mount Cargill were repeated as she and others of Scottish descent, in an act of repentance and reconciliation, asked forgiveness on behalf of the city forefathers for not including Maori in their Calvinistic structure. The younger generation honored Violet and prayed for her. Violet then prayed for the TX members. As the strongmen went on stage, I need not have asked her how she was; the determined gleam in her eye said it all. "This is one of the best days of my life," she said.

It was also one of the best days for Hamilton coordinator, Michael Lo-Schuemperli, who had flown from Hamilton to attend the Dunedin TX night with his father. When Kevin Stark asked for those who wanted to respond to Christ to come forward, Mike turned to his father and asked, "Dad, what about it? Will you give Jesus a chance to change your life?"

His father replied, "I think He already has, but let's go forward." An overjoyed Mike was able to walk forward with his father, and a gray-haired counselor was ideally suited to leading his father to Christ.

I believe that God loves families and delights to unite and reconcile them. I was touched by the large numbers of family members that responded to the gospel message either as a direct result of their family involvement in the tour or as a ripple effect. There were many cases around the country of individuals responding to Christ and then bringing along other family members on subsequent evenings. Immediately prior to the IWT events, a couple had separated. The mother and daughter attended the TX evening, and both responded at the altar call. The father and son attended the second night and came forward. On the GX night the whole family rededicated themselves to the Lord and to one another, happy, satisfied, and reconciled. One father brought all eight of his children on stage after a performance; they all wanted to follow Christ.

A middle-aged woman driving a small car arrived unnoticed by the crowd, and because of the rain and thunder, she chose to stay in her car. Her nephew, Ray Totorewa, leader of Island Breeze, New Zealand, was preaching for the first time on the tour that night at Aitarahiki Marae, near Timaru. As Ray prayed the prayer of salvation, tears streamed down his aunt's face as she prayed along with him, although she did not feel comfortable responding physically to an altar call. She later sent a phone text message to Ray with the good news that she had become a believer.

Similarly, thirty-eight of the Maori and Polynesian Island Breeze team experienced the joy of family members from different towns around the county responding to Christ during the tour.

Testimonies from the South Island

It's time to see what God has in store for us

An eleven-year-old girl and her mother came forward at GX to receive salvation. "It's time to see what God has in store for us," the mother said.

From China

Jak, an eighteen-year-old Chinese student who arrived a week before IWT came to town, had been asking many questions about Christianity and had read the Bible his host had given him. When he attended Island Breeze, he went forward to become a Christian. Immediately he called his father in China, only to be met with a cool reception. "We have our own religion, Jak," the father said.

Jak is meeting with some other Chinese Christian students to help him in his newfound faith.

From Jehovah's Witness to faith in Christ

A fifty-year-old Chinese man had been attending a Jehovah's Witness church. As a counselor explained the price that Jesus paid for him on the cross, he came to faith in Christ and began attending one of the churches sponsoring IWT.

A personal relationship with her Savior

A twenty-eight-year-old woman wept as she came forward at the altar call. Although she had been attending church, she did not know she could have a personal relationship with her Savior, Jesus.

They rededicated their lives

A young married couple wept as they rededicated their lives to Christ.

You taught me to trust in Jesus

"You taught me to trust in Jesus. You showed me that Jesus died on the cross for me. Now I have a real life, not a life of selfishness and laziness. I made lots of bad choices, but now I am free. I loved the Impact World Tour."

A student rededicates his life to Christ

"I've been struggling because I'm living in Studentville down in Dunedin. I'm surrounded by guys who like to party all the time and drink. It's hard. I don't think it will be easier, but I'll keep trying."

Chapter Sixteen

Finishing Up

Not unto us, O Lord, not unto us, but to Your name give glory.

Psalm 115:1

As the entire crew commenced their two-day northward journey from Dunedin to Northland for the final week of the Proclamation Phase, excitement increased in Kaitaia, the most northern city hosting IWT. Many of the Kaitaia pastors had been praying together for several years and had held regular retreats in Northland. They quickly saw the potential for IWT to be part of the answer to their prayer to share the gospel in the whole district, and the Executive Task Force, chaired by Jim Patrick, did everything possible to ensure the smooth running of the campaign. There was a certain advantage in being in the last week of the tour, since some earlier logistical problems had been resolved. Although there were some problems with drugs, the crowds were mostly well controlled. During the campaign nights, police worked closely with IWT organizers.

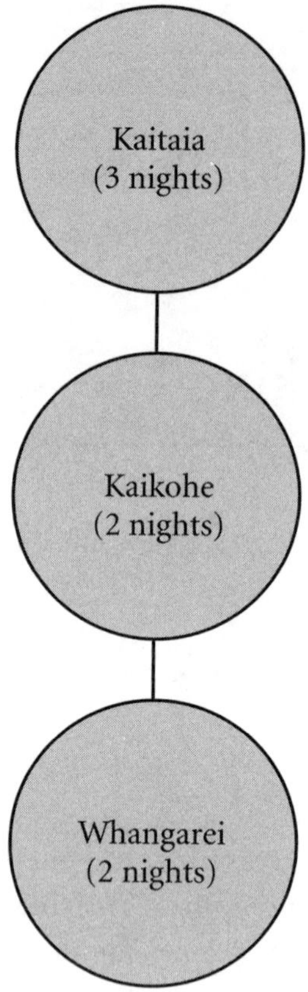

A total of eight thousand people, approximately 40 percent of the region's population, came from the northern tip of New Zealand and from many rural areas to attend the campaign nights.

Jason Hotere, who was born in the Northland town of Hokianga, desired to preach to his own people more than anywhere else. As he introduced himself in Kaitaia as a hometown boy from the Ngapuhi tribe, the crowd roared with approval. When he shared his testimony and preached the gospel, a great quietness settled. "You could have heard a pin drop on the grass," Jason said later. Jason struck a chord with the crowds while sharing his testimony, as Northland has one of the highest suicide rates nationally. All the teams contributed greatly to restoring hope in the community, and a total of 529 people responded at altar calls.

Right until the end of the tour, however, we had to allow for things that could go wrong. When the clutch of the truck hauling the ramps from the South Island failed near Taihape, in the middle of the North Island, we realized it would be impossible to move the ramps to Northland in time for the GX program the following evening. I called Jay, the tour director in Kaikohe, and said, "Jay, we can't get those ramps up for Kaikohe tomorrow evening. You're going to have to get some other ramps." I knew Jay's struggle to get those ramps manufactured and understood his reluctance to get another set at this stage, so I appreciated his response.

"Are you sure we can't get another truck and trailer?"

"No," I replied emphatically. "Andy has tried everything. Nothing is available at this short notice." Jay managed to unload a five-meter trailer and borrow some much smaller ramps in Auckland. I did not think we would need these ramps when they were offered to us earlier on. Jay and the ramps arrived in Kaikohe, completing setup as the rain stopped, with five minutes left to check technical gear. No one would have known about the last-minute scramble as the GX team again gave their all in sharing the love of God.

For the final two nights in Whangarei, the teams put on their best effort for the finish of the tour. As in the other northern towns, a large percentage of Maori were among two hundred people who came forward at the altar call. One woman in her mid-forties had made a commitment to Christ twenty years before but had found it difficult to reconcile her Maori culture with her faith in Christ. "When I saw those

Maori people and Maori dancers," she said, smiling, "I realized I could return to my faith in Christ."

Many other people were standing around, just watching.

The ramp and tech teams found extra reserves of energy as they cheerfully packed down the gear for the last time. As the crowds left, I could hardly believe this part of the tour was over. I felt like the first part of a good movie had finished, and I wanted to savor every memory—the victories and battles, the intense prayer, crowds of young people and families standing with heads bowed at altars around the country, and the thousands of believers who had expended themselves in this venture.

One woman who had loved working on the hospitality team with Christians from other churches echoed my thoughts, "You know, Dave, the only thing wrong with IWT is that it is finished! We so enjoyed working with all the churches!"

I replied, "It's not finished. Only the proclamation phase has finished. So much is only just beginning."

Thursday, April 8, 2004

The following day was the Thursday before Good Friday, 2004. All teams associated with the tour, together with our IWT staff, gathered for a final meal before the international staff left the country. We met in the courtyard of the South Auckland YWAM property, where we had rallied during the Boot Camp at the commencement of the tour three months. Flags from the many represented nations hung from the ceiling.

The courtyard hummed with raucous laughter and rising voices as old and new friends from the tour greeted and hugged one another, exchanging their favorite stories and memories from the tour. We had much to celebrate in considering the outcomes of the tour.

Outcomes—Harvest and Discipleship

- Approximately 315,000 heard an uncompromising gospel message at main events
- 700,000+ heard the gospel through television coverage
- 12,654 people made first-time responses to Christ
- 23,565 people in total responded to Christ
- Approximately 2,000 responded to Christ in pre-tour events (2003)

Outcomes—Events

- 15 hub and 35 satellite venues
- 200 major performances
- 400 school performances
- 25 performances in 10 prisons
- 3 national television appearances
- 540,000 "free" tickets distributed

I stood alone, surveying the gathering. Many of our staff were enjoying the celebration after the hard work of the last three years. Jenny commented, "I can't believe we did it, but we did!" Brian Kleinsasser reported that once all the accounts were settled, we even had a small financial surplus to sow into other IWT endeavors. Our young staff had risen to areas of responsibility that they never would have imagined. Almost all of them had a greater understanding of how they could reach their generation with the love of God. Many of our staff would continue to pursue that goal. Right now it was time to "Enjoy and Rejoice!"

These three words resonated so strongly in my spirit. Frank Eijengraam, our Hutt Valley coordinator, felt the Lord speak these words quietly to him as he wandered around the Lower Hutt Reserve after the performing teams left. He was wondering what lay ahead for him and the city in which he had labored.

After the long and hard hours, the travail and battles we had all endured, it was a time to rejoice and to rest.

As the evening proceeded, leaders of the performing team summarized their impressions of the tour.

Kevin Stark, the leader of TX and veteran of over thirty-five tours, felt the people of the land warmly received the teams. "Many said this tour couldn't be done," he said. "But as the church, YWAM, and people of all cultures picked up the vision, we saw lives changed in towns all over New Zealand."

Ray and Shaneane Totorewa spoke of the joy it was to see family members of all of their New Zealand Island Breeze team members respond to Christ. "We were also delighted to see Maori and people from many cultures respond positively to various cultural components of the tour."

Jesse Fellers from GX came to the microphone. "Physically," he said, "this has been a crazy tour, but we give thanks to God for all He has done. We have seen thousands of kids coming to Christ. We have already heard of some young people that came forward at altar calls during the tour influencing their friends with the gospel message. I believe we will see a ripple effect into other nations as a result of this tour."

Toward the close of the evening, we all cheered loudly for the ramp and tech crews who had worked so hard over the months of the tour.

Finally, late in the night, we all turned our thanksgiving and the loudest applause for the evening to the Lord, who had made IWT possible and for all He had done. What an incredible adventure of faith the last three years had been! It had begun with a small seed of faith sown in Mark Anderson's heart ten years ago, had multiplied into the hearts of hundreds of volunteers and intercessors, and was reaped as a wonderful harvest over those last three months. I am sure my praise and thanksgiving was the loudest in the courtyard.

Chapter Seventeen

Aftermath

God never intended Impact World Tour to be a series of interesting, vital events but rather a Holy Spirit–directed and energized movement that would be a catalyst to launch the beachhead for genuine revival throughout the land.

Joy Dawson[1]

Fruit That Remains

With every harvest comes the seed that will multiply for the next harvest. While we could not presume that all who responded at altar calls during IWT would become lifelong followers of Jesus Christ, we heard many testimonies of those whose lives had changed dramatically as a result.

One seventeen-year-old committed his life to the Lord during the TX International night in Masterton and was tragically killed in an accident one month after the campaign. During that time, although he had not felt comfortable in any discipleship group, he was, however, regularly reading his Bible and testified to many of his friends of the power of Jesus Christ to change lives. He counseled a few of them against suicide. Some family members were impacted by his transformed life and death and were also keen to find the passion he had.

We saw many signs of those whose lives had been touched during the tour beginning to reach out to others. Our daughter Lisa came home from an afternoon at the beach and told us how a teenager who had responded to Christ at IWT eagerly began to share her newfound faith with her. She also observed a group of six boys gather around a young leader at Subway, clutching their *Real Life* New Testaments.

One Maori man, together with two family members, in a rural community made a commitment during IWT. While he still struggled with his family's addictive patterns, he made progress, and children and teenagers from his *whanau* (family) became actively involved in church activities.

Around the nation, discipleship groups for children and youth flourished. In the small town of Opunake, some high school girls who became believers during the tour started a lunchtime discipleship group at their high school, the first time in many years that a Christian group had been active within the school grounds. In the Hutt Valley, several youth groups grew significantly; one continued to grow after IWT, increasing from approximately fifty to sixty members to over one hundred and fifty.

Even twelve months later we continued to hear reports of people who responded at altar calls during IWT and influenced their friends. One boy from Freeport, Illinois, USA, gave his heart to Christ on the first day of his family holiday in New Zealand. When IWT came to Illinois a year later, he was there, grinning and supporting his friends who responded to Christ at the altar call.

Despite these reports, discipleship proved to be one of the more difficult areas in the immediate aftermath of the campaign. We had always tried to communicate to pastors and leaders that even a large response at altar calls would not necessarily translate into an immediate influx of new believers into the churches the following Sunday. Rather we encouraged ongoing discipleship in a context that met the needs of new believers within a familiar culture.

I observed that where young people had an existing connection to something Christian, they were more prepared to become involved in church or youth group. Small groups that worked well were those where the members already had good relationships with unbelievers.

As I See It

The final numbers of those who truly responded will not be known until the day of Christ. Yet we know that besides those who came forward, there were many who were deeply touched. Scores of people, many probably for the first time, would have heard the message of a God who loved them so much that He sent His Son to die for them. They heard again and again, through the real, life-changing testimonies of people like Jason Hotere and many others, of a God who can and will forgive and set them free from the bondage and curse of sin. God's Word never returns empty. Many more will ultimately hear the call and be saved.

The fruit of this event cannot be measured or counted. Good trees will continue to bear fruit and multiply. Even one small seed has the potential to multiply beyond measure, let alone the many that responded during the tour.

Although Impact World Tour is clearly a tool in the hand of God, it's not an end in itself; it's only the beginning of even greater things to come!

Hank Overeem

The statistics do not really do justice to the impact the campaigns had at a local community level. In the aftermath of IWT, I was amazed at the increase in prayer around the country. The boost of international prayer through the International House of Prayer involvement was noticeable. When this was added to local and national prayer, it lifted the campaigns to a whole new level. Some networks that were formed during IWT continued to meet after the tour. Reconciliation initiatives and prayer initiatives were all beginning simultaneously in different locations and in different streams of the New Zealand church. The national leaders of the Salvation Army, for example, commissioned a whole year from March 2005 to a commitment to 24/7 prayer throughout their ranks. Other church streams were looking at similar proposals. God continues to stir His people to pray.

Reports of increased unity also came from many places after the tour. Vision Net New Zealand, a national network of the evangelical churches in New Zealand, currently led by Glyn Carpenter, a former businessman, has been assisting in seeing greater cooperation and unity across the New Zealand church in recent years. He remarked to me, "Dave, if there was an award for helping advances in unity in the body of Christ at this time, I would give it to IWT from what I have seen across the nation."

Testimonies

Momentum in our combined youth network

> *We got momentum back in our combined youth network. As a youth pastor, I got to work with pastors in other churches that I had never worked with before.*
>
> *Youth Pastor*

A vehicle of sufficient size and value

IWT increased unity by providing a vehicle of sufficient size and value to gather around.

Usher/Security Chair

Otherwise unconnected

IWT required many churches in our city, otherwise unconnected, to pray together, plan together, train together, and minister together. IWT was able to iron out some of the theological and denominational differences that divide our fellowships and facilitate fruitful, cooperative ministry.

Youth Taskforce Chair

It is not a time for the New Zealand church to draw back but rather run through the break in the battle lines while a breach has been made through IWT and other initiatives. We must continue to deepen alliances and friendships formed or strengthened through the tour. We must seek God for His ongoing strategies for influencing our communities in every sphere. The church must continue to advance on every front.

Going Deeper

Now Is the Time

A vision for revival has been proclaimed and served by many noble people such as evangelist Muri Thompson, ministry pioneer Neville Winger, and prophetic teacher Campbell McAlpine. Through many such faithful lives, the stage has been set for the turning of this nation to God. The Impact World Tour has been a necessary part of this preparation. City after city had to come together in common vision.

Towns and districts once dislocated through indifference or division now contain alliances of Christian leaders who have come together in a spirit of friendship and respect. Like the bones that came together in Ezekiel's vision of Israel (Ezekiel 37), God is calling us to align with each other in order to become a community filled with the living breath of His Spirit. Now is the time.

John Dawson

The church in New Zealand has been reawakened to the openness of this generation to the gospel when it is preached in a relevant way. Thousands of counselors are now better equipped to share their faith with others. Jung Bee, our Korean facilitator in Auckland, said to me, "IWT maximized and brought out what was already in our young people. Every week they now go into the city, using hip hop, breakdance, and contemporary music to reach out to other youth."

Members of each of the performing teams have remained in New Zealand to continue to work in evangelism with different communities. They will also assist in forthcoming campaigns in the Pacific and Asia.

In Hutt Valley, a core group of business, church, ministry, and community leaders, brought together during IWT, continued to meet together, sometimes with prayer and fasting. This team has carried on working in unity to develop long-term strategies to impact their city. One of their goals is to promote Christians who are active in each sphere of society to meet, pray, and strategize together how to best impact their sphere with Christian values. The eight spheres of society they want to influence are family, education, business, youth and children, local government, community and social services, media, and arts and entertainment.

Come and Help Us

Ripples resulting from the tour in New Zealand spread quickly to other nations.

In early December 2004 at the University of the Nations in Kona, Hawaii, Sue and I joined other international leaders of IWT, together with leaders of the university and other members of the body of Christ. Three representative leaders from Fiji were also present, including Ratu Osea Gavidi,[2] a Fijian chief and well-respected, godly kingdom builder over many years. The Fijians desired to see the whole of their nation rebuilt and transformed.

Our meetings culminated at the new outdoor auditorium on the University campus. While we enjoyed the warm Hawaiian breeze, Ratu Osea, accompanied by the Fijian contingent, presented the highest form of honor, the whale's tooth, to Loren Cunningham. Then, from his heart, while on his knees, he made a formal plea in his own language to the University of the Nations to help in rebuilding Fiji, to see Christians established in every sphere of society. Ratu Osea had been through the same process as Nehemiah had, first of public repentance, then of calling the church to rebuild the walls that had been broken down in every sphere of society—government, education, and business. Loren Cunningham, speaking on behalf of YWAM, responded, "We will come. We will come to Fiji." As Loren presented a canoe oar to Ratu Osea, he made it clear that our response in YWAM would be to honor the tribal chiefs in Fiji and the leaders of the church denominations as "steersmen of the canoe." We would come in recognition of the Fijian leadership and serve where possible. In a formal response, representatives from different nations, dressed in national costume, came on stage and, speaking in their native languages, declared their willingness to serve in Fiji. Nations represented included Samoa, Algeria, New Zealand, Spain, Korea, China, Saudi Arabia, India, and Taiwan.

Fijian Taubale Toki, who had worked on the New Zealand campaign since early 2001, returned to Fiji in May 2005 and began preparation for IWT in 2006. We believe Fiji is a hub for the future of the Pacific campaigns and that the process of reconciliation and restoration that has begun in Fiji can provide keys of release for other Pacific Islands.

Australian YWAM leaders in Perth, Western Australia, and in Townsville, North Queensland, took up the challenge of hosting IWT in their respective states, beginning in 2006. We believe they can build on what has happened in New Zealand. Requests are also coming from other islands of the Pacific and nations in Asia for proclamation of the gospel through IWT.

In many ways, IWT New Zealand has been a laboratory, a place of new beginnings. The effects of the nationwide tour have ramifications that extend beyond the shores of this land. God's dream is to reach every nation, every people, and every generation in every area with the truth of the gospel. We *all* have a part to play in this.

Postscript

Tauranga, October 2005

Sue and I were busily placing our week's groceries in the supermarket cart. In a remarkable series of events, beginning with my nocturnal meeting with a Tauranga doctor during IWT, we put aside our plans to return to Asia. At the invitation of a small group of pastors and leaders, we moved instead to Tauranga. We planned to help pioneer a House of Prayer in the city that would eventually lead 24/7 prayer and worship. We also planned a resource and command mission center for evangelism campaigns in the Pacific and Asia region. These initiatives were to be built on the foundations of unity and prayer that had been laid over many years and brought to clear focus through the IWT campaign period.

The ash blonde checkout clerk chatted to us as she scanned the items.

"Are you watching the rugby match tonight?" she asked.

"Rugby?" I repeated. I had forgotten it was on. I glanced at Sue. "No," I said. "I've promised my wife to work on something tonight." I noticed that Sue looked relieved.

"What's that?" the checkout girl asked. "Everybody in New Zealand is watching the rugby final."

"We're working on a book," I mumbled, not expecting her to be interested. I was leaving for IWT preparation meetings in Fiji and Australia the following week and knew that I had to complete the final draft before I left.

"What sort of book?" she persisted.

I paused. "Have you ever heard of Impact World Tour? We're writing the story."

"Impact World Tour!" she exclaimed. Her face lit up. "That changed my life."

"Really?" I asked, intrigued.

"Yes," she said. "Mum used to take me to church as a kid. Impact World Tour was the thing that made me give my heart to Jesus. I started going back to church after that."

"How are you getting on now?" I asked.

"Great!" she said, smiling. "You would have never thought it, but I am now a youth leader and Sunday school teacher in our church."

"That's wonderful." I said while paying for the groceries. "Keep it up."

As we drove off, our groceries in the car, Sue looked at me. "That's really what Impact World Tour is all about, isn't it, Dave? Young people like that checkout clerk being changed by the gospel, then influencing those around them."

"Yes," I said. "Who knows how many youth whose lives have been touched through IWT will go out and impact their world for Jesus."

I thought of the prayer and outreach initiatives continuing in many communities in New Zealand and the ripple effect of the nationwide tours in Australia, Fiji, and eventually other nations.

"And," I added, "it's also about impacting our communities and other nations with the gospel."

Appendix A

Biblical Principles of Praying for New Zealand

By Joy Dawson

Since 1956, God has called me to biblically based, fervent intercession, many times with fasting, for genuine revival and spiritual awakening to come to New Zealand. And for decades my husband, Jim, and I have partnered together on a weekly basis to cry out to God for this awesome visitation of the Holy Spirit that would shake the whole nation in unprecedented ways. We have understood that genuine revival cannot be contained or sustained without an adherence to biblical principles. This led us to regularly intercede for the following:

1. For God to raise up apostles, prophets, evangelists, pastors, and teachers throughout the land from among the Maoris, the Islanders, and the whites (Ephesians 4:11).

2. That they would fulfill the conditions of being empowered by the Holy Spirit on a daily basis (Ephesians 5:18).
3. That they would operate in the fear of the Lord, releasing them from the fear of man, living holy, Christlike lives (Proverbs 8:13).
4. That they would study the character and ways of God from His Word and then live by them and teach them (Jeremiah 9:23, 24; Exodus 33:13).
5. That they would seek God for His vision for the spheres of authority and influence He would release to them and lead the people accordingly (Proverbs 29:1).
6. That God would raise up unifiers in the body of Christ and that His people would see the necessity of being united, in gender, denominationally, racially, and generationally, for the purpose of evangelizing and discipling the lost.
7. That God would reveal to the spiritual leaders and the people that the unity Jesus prayed for in John 17:23 is not only the greatest tool for evangelism; without it, the church will be totally ineffective (Matthew 12:25).
8. That God would reveal to all that they are totally ineffective without the love of God operating through them (1 Corinthians 13:1), and that they are only as loving as they are humble. So humility is the greatest need for biblical unity (Philippians 2:1-3).
9. That God would move by His Spirit upon all of His people to seek Him for a *burdened heart for the lost,* with the understanding that this is the key that motivates a true soul-winner. We are not following Jesus if we are not bringing people to Christ, as a way of life, according to Matthew 4:19.
10. That God would put righteous, God-fearing, Bible-believing leaders into all spheres of authority and influence throughout the land (Proverbs 29:2).

11. That the Bible would have its rightful place in the nation, that it would be the basis of the laws, and that it would be read, understood, and believed in as the inspired Word of God and applied to people's lives (2 Timothy 3:16; Psalm 119:26).
12. That God would raise up radically real youth leaders who have a passion to know God and to make Him known and that He would bring forth a revolution of righteousness among the youth of New Zealand (Isaiah 45:8; Isaiah 62:1).
13. That God would thrust forth laborers from New Zealand into the nations of the world in unprecedented numbers, whose lives reflect the above biblical principles (Matthew 9:38).
14. That every believer's goal would be to submit to the Holy Spirit's dealings to be conformed to the image of the Lord Jesus (Romans 12:29) and to have a passion for God to be glorified at all times (Psalm 115:1).
15. That God would stir up the body of Christ in New Zealand to understand the incredible privilege of partnering with the Head of the church, the Lord Jesus Christ, in His priestly, priority role as Chief Intercessor; and that they would choose to become history-shapers of the nation by engaging in the same ministry, under the Spirit's direction.

In my understanding, Impact World Tour is a direct answer to those many, many prayers. From the first time I heard about Impact World Tour, New Zealand, in 1999, near the inception of the vision, God graced my husband and me with an unusually deep burden for the fulfillment of this vision. I can only say that I have been compelled to pray with urgency, intensity, persistency, and strong faith.

Through IWT, God is giving the church in New Zealand an opportunity to know that "this is your hour of visitation." We believe that God will so stir and unite the body of Christ that they will testify as Job did, "*You have granted [us] life and favor, and Your care has preserved [our] spirit*" (Job 10:12).

Jim and I have incorporated all of the above aspects of interceding for New Zealand over the decades into our intercession for IWT over the past five years. But there are additional aspects that need sharing.

We have majored in crying out to God that the sharing of the gospel would include the need for repentance of sin, not just confession, and that the cost of discipleship would be made clear. We are convinced God wants to have many of the new converts thoroughly discipled and then sent out to make God known to the nations of the world. It's part of God's overall vision, and we long for and pray that it will not be aborted by short-changing the people with how Jesus presented His claims, at the price of having more statistics to share related to responses to the altar calls.

Being geographically further removed than most other countries from the rest of the world's turmoil, and surrounded by such an abundance of natural beauty and plenty, New Zealanders are tempted to become complacent, in fact apathetic. Subsequently we have found ourselves battling in warfare prayer against this force.

We have also not been surprised at the battle in prayer related to the need for finances to be released from God's people for the fulfillment of the IWT vision. As New Zealand citizens, we understand this. It took our coming to live in the USA as missionaries at the call of God in 1971 to see how much we needed to learn about God's perspective on money. We were already consistent tithers. The effect was revolutionary and wonderfully liberating—in fact, life changing.

We are also aware that a strong stand needs to be taken to maintain effective intercession after IWT teams have left the country. God never intended IWT to be a series of interesting, vital events but rather a Holy Spirit–directed and energized movement that would be a catalyst to launch the beachhead for genuine revival throughout the land.

Isaiah 66:7-9 tells us that a land is not "born in a day" (NIV), a child is not born without travail. But after the desperate, determined, diligent, united cries of intercessors who will not let God go and who will keep giving God no rest and no peace, heaven's flood gates will open. The deluge will be released. Hosea 6:3 will be fulfilled. "*As surely as the sun rises, he will appear; he will come to us like the winter rains, like the spring rains that water the earth*" (NIV).

We must release the praise of faith that just as God promises in Isaiah 66:9—there will be no still births to our spiritual travail—so God promised that the nations at the end of the earth will have a mighty visitation of the Spirit of God. "*The Lord will lay bare His holy arm in the sight of all nations, and all the ends of the earth will see the salvation of our God*" (Isaiah 52:10 NIV).

Committed to that cause,
Joy Dawson

Appendix B

Counselor Training

During two counselor training sessions, counselor trainers used the following basic outline, although each trainer expressed it differently, according to his or her gifts and personality.

Session A—The Message and the Messenger

1. The Message

This session emphasizes the essentials of the gospel message, including the Lordship of Christ.

God's plan

Fact: God's original plan for mankind was that we would have life and that life would be lived in the fellowship of His Presence.

Our problem

Fact: Through Adam and Eve's disobedience, sin entered the world and separated all mankind from God. Our unrighteousness condemns us as guilty of sin and deserving of the same just punishment. The punishment for sin is death.

Read: Romans 6:23a, Isaiah 64:6, Deuteronomy 24:16, Romans 3:23, Romans 5:12, Romans 8:7-8, Ephesians 2:1-3

Remember: Our *sin* has separated us from life with God and the punishment for our sin is *death.*

God's solution

Fact: God sent His Son into the world to bear the punishment for our sins. He became the perfect, sinless sacrifice, substituted on our behalf. His death fulfilled the justice requirements of God's righteous law and freed us from the judgment of death. His resurrection gives us life.

Read: Romans 3:25-26, Romans 5:6, John 3:16, 2 Corinthians 5:21, 1 Peter 3:18, Ephesians 1:7-8, Romans 5:10, Romans 6: 4-10

Remember: Jesus Christ, sinless and perfect, died in our place and paid the price completely for our sin.

Our response

Fact: If by faith we call upon the name of Jesus Christ, trusting in Him for salvation, and acknowledging our sin with true repentance, we will be saved.

Read: 1 John 1:9, Romans 10:9-11, Romans 3:22-24, Romans 5:1-2, John 6:40, John 18:6, Luke 9:23-26

Remember: Salvation comes through *repentance* and *faith* in Jesus Christ.

Conclusion

Fact: God sent His Son into the world to reconcile His lost creation—mankind—back to Himself. His desire is that we would have life and live in the fellowship of His Presence; it always has been and it always will be.

2. The Messenger—Lordship of Christ

Fact: We are called to live our life "in Christ." That means:

- Surrendering to His will
- Living for His glory
- Growing in grace and the knowledge of Him

Read: Galatians 6:14, Romans 6:19-22, Romans 12:1-3, 1 Corinthians 2:2, Philippians 3:7-10, Romans 8:1-4.

Remember: "You are not your own, you were bought at a price" (1 Corinthians 6:19).

Differences between living wholeheartedly for the Lord (in the Spirit) and living for ourselves (in the flesh) are explained. Concepts of salvation by faith and sanctification are explained

Session B—The Mechanics

1. Why Do We Need to Disciple the Inquirers?

a. In Matthew 28:19-20, Jesus said, "Therefore go and make disciples of all nations, baptizing them in the name of the Father and of the Son and of the Holy Spirit, and teaching them to obey everything I have commanded you" (NIV).

Engel Scale

God's Role	Church's Role			
			-10	Awareness of supernatural
			-9	No knowledge of Christianity
	Presence		-8	Initial awareness of Christianity
Conviction			-7	Interest in Christianity
			-6	Awareness of basics of the gospel
	Proclamation		-5	Grasp of implications of the Bible
		Rejection	-4	Positive attitudes to the gospel
	Persuasion		-3	Awareness of personal need
			-2	Challenge and decision to act
Regeneration			-1	Repentance and faith
NEW BIRTH				**JOHN 3:3**
Sanctification			1	Evaluation of decision
			2	Initiation into the church
			3	Beginning to disciple others
			4	Growth in understanding & faith
			5	Growth in Christian character
			6	Discovery and use of gifts
			7	Christian lifestyle
			8	Stewardship of resources
			9	Prayer
			10	Openness to others
			11	Effective sharing of faith & life

b. Engel Scale—the development of a Christian. Discipleship is a process as people learn about God and get to know Him.

c. The need for relationship: You don't leave a new baby to fend for itself. If you just take care of its needs but don't love it and cuddle it, it will die. We need to nurture and care for new believers in the same way.

d. Development of relationship—so that people come into a place of trust, where they can share their needs and have them met. People generally come forward to have Jesus meet a need in their life. We may need to help them see Jesus meet their needs.

2. Sharing Your Testimony

During this session, counsellors are trained to share their testimony of how they came to Christ and how their life changed as a result.

3. Sharing the Gospel Using the Tract

Counsellors are shown how to use the "New Life" gospel tract used with enquirers. They are also encouraged to use part of their own testimony, as appropriate. Time is given for practice.

4. Instructions for Counsellors

Practical instructions are given to counsellors in the whole process of counselling during an altar call and immediate follow-up. A practice altar call is given.

Appendix C

Statistics from the Tour

Date	City - Venue	City Size	Attendance	Total per city
Jan 22-24	Gisborne - Awapuni Stadium	33,000	10,000	736
28-Jan	Marton - Memorial Hall	5,000	950	174
28-Jan	Opunake - Sandford Events Centre	1,500	1,037	151
Jan 29-31	Hawera - Hicks Park Rugby Ground	11,000	3,400	217
Jan 29-31	Wanganui - Cooks Garden Stadium	46,000	11,200	617
	Kaitoki Prison	46,000	60	8
31-Jan	Patea - The Domain	700	250	48
Feb 5-7	Dannevirke - The Domain	5,500	4,000	313
Feb 5-7	Hastings - Nelson Park	120,000	18,500	1094
10-Feb	Kapiti Coast - Coastlands Carpark	30,000	2,500	151
11-Feb	Upper Hutt - Expressions, Arts & Entertainment Center	36,000	1,200	174

Feb 12-14	Hutt City - Hutt Recreation Grounds	150,000	11,000	758
Feb 13-14	Masterton - Colin Pugh Sports Bowl	30,000	4,400	330
Feb 17-18	Porirua City - Hartham Place	47,000	4,200	256
	Rimutaka prison + Wellington prison - various pres.		523	189
20-Feb	Hutt City - Walter Nash Stadium	150,000	2,000	339
Feb 19-21	Wellington City - Basin Reserve	150,000	7,432	678
20-Feb	Foxton - Eastern Park	10,000	1,200	127
Feb 24-25	Matamata - Bedford Park	6,000	4,200	376
25-Feb	Motueka - Decks Reserve	6,000	2,000	66
Feb 26-28	Nelson -Trafalgar Park/ Nelson Boys College (indoor) - 2 shows	60,000	7,800	659
Feb 27-28	Whakatane - RUGBY PARK/ War Memorial Hall - 2 shows (indoor)	17,000	7,500	475
Feb 26-28	Blenheim - Anchor Stadium	20,000	6,800	673
Feb 27-28	Paeroa - domain/ War Memorial Hall - 2 shows (indoor)		2,275	207
Mar 01-03	Te Awamutu - Racecourse	8,000	7,360	467
Mar 02-04	Tauranga - Western Bay Finance Stadium	97,000	18,500	1260
Mar 04-06	Hamilton - Waikato Stadium	120,000	19,900	1029
Mar-03	Huntly College	7,000	1,050	124
Mar 4-6	Tokoroa - Memorial Sports Ground	8,000	7,200	460
Mar 5-6	Raglan - Raglan Area School	3,500	1,080	105
Mar 9-10	Central Auckland - Takaparawha Park, Bastion Point	1,800,000	4,500	390
Mar 12-13	Auckland - Northshore Events Centre	1,800,000	7,900	766
Mar 12-13	West Auckland - Parrs Park, Glenn Eden	1,800,000	10,000	673
Mar 15-17	South Auckland - Massey Park, Papakura	1,800,000	13,800	688
Mar 17-19	Auckland, Supertop Ericsson Stadium	1,800,000	16,800	1436
Mar 19-20	Hibiscus Coast, Stanmore Bay Park		6,500	411

Mar-20	Helensville, Parakai Domain	3,000	1,300	122
Mar 24-26	Rangiora A&P show grounds, New Life Christian School	10,000	8,320	454
Mar 25-27	Christchurch - Westpac Centre	350,000	19,935	2193
Mar-24	Timaru - Sound Shell, Caroline Bay	38,000	2,500	293
Mar-25	Leeston - Rugby Ground, High Street	2,500	950	194
Mar-26	Reefton - Race Course	1,000	900	104
Mar 29-30	Invercargil - Stadium Southland	50,000	10,300	739
Mar-30	Cromwell - Anderson Park	2,500	450	69
Mar31-Apr 1	Oamaru - Centennial Park	13,500	5,200	414
Mar 31-Apr2	Alexandra - Molyneux Park	4,500	2,650	325
Apr 1-3	Dunedin - Forbury Park Raceway	110,000	19,000	941
Apr 5-7	Kaitaia - A&P Showgrounds	10,000	7,800	529
Apr 5-6	Kaikohe - Rugby Grounds	6,000	4,500	332
Apr 6-7	Whangerei - I.T.M. Stadium	20,000	3,785	334
		TOTALS	316,607	23,668
	Percentage of New Zealand reached (4.2 million people)		4,200,000	
	TV Show "Holmes" - 3 min. Gospel presentation by TX		500,000	

Hubs	13
Satellites	33

Total Response by Age

Category	*Total*	*% of Total*
Under 13 Male	4673	25.52
Under 13 Female	3696	20.18
13-18 Male	3978	21.72
13-18 Female	3992	21.80
19-25 Male	494	2.69
19-25 Female	509	2.80
26-35 Male	188	1.03
26-35 Female	283	1.54
36-50 Male	143	0.78
36-50 Female	224	1.22
51+ Male	61	0.33
51+ Female	73	0.39
	18,314	100

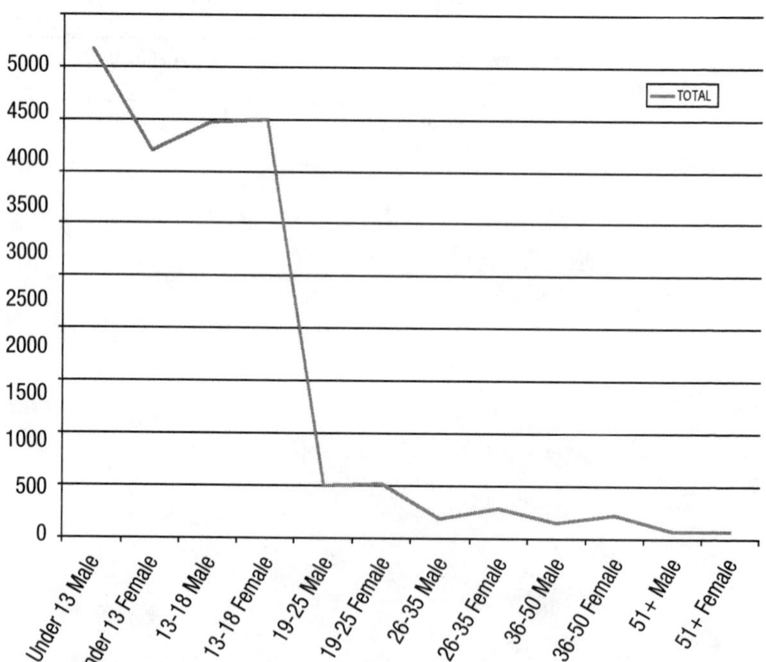

Photographs from the Tour

Impact World Tour – A "Catalyst" in Tauranga

"We're going after unchurched people"

GISBORNE, the first city in the world to see the sunrise each day, will also be the first city to host Impact World Tour (IWT) New Zealand, the country's largest nationwide evangelistic campaign in many years. The Tour launches in Gisborne in January, and recently the city saw a glimpse of what lies on the horizon.

On August 29, two members of Team Xtreme performed for a packed house in the Lytton High School Hall. "It was a great atmosphere," says Gary Stevenson, pastor of Gisborne Assembly of God and executive chairperson for Gisborne IWT. "They had a tremendous rapport with the audience."

Spectators cheered as Jason Hotere of New Zealand and Rick Vannatta from the United States broke stacks of concrete bricks, bent metal bars with their bare hands, and blew up hot water bottles.

But the true success of the night was revealed when an

High-impact extravaganz

IWT heats up in Nelson and Marlborough

"New Zealand hasn't seen anything like this in a long time."

Other Nelson Team Xtreme appearances included presentations at Waimea and Nelson Colleges.

Blenheim also hosted a Burn service in October with Team Xtreme, held at Marlborough Centre. Over 250 youth attended, from many different churches in the area – a very encouraging turnout for an area where, in the past five years, it has been difficult to achieve attendance high-

Strong Christian message

By MELANIE GLOVER

Xtreme message after extremes in weather

By Helen Harvey

WHAT'S ON

Free shows deliver action, message about right choic

extreme sports

Impact World Tour will hit NZ this summer. Performers from all over the world are here to participate in world class skateboarding demos, hip hop dances, Maori and Pacific Island cultural performances, athletic and strongman power demonstrations, and more.

'Muscle with a message'

Crowds thrilled by high-flying stuntmen

By ANNA BOWDEN

Enthusiastic response to IWT

treme

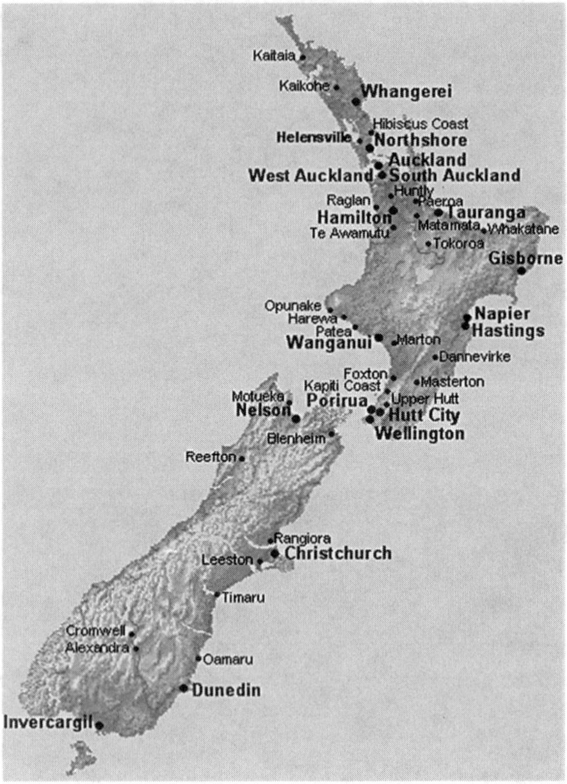
Kaitaia
Kaikohe
Whangerei
Hibiscus Coast
Helensville
Northshore
Auckland
West Auckland
South Auckland
Huntly
Raglan
Paeroa
Hamilton
Tauranga
Matamata
Whakatane
Te Awamutu
Tokoroa
Gisborne
Opunake
Harewa
Patea
Napier
Hastings
Wanganui
Marton
Dannevirke
Foxton
Kapiti Coast
Masterton
Motueka
Porirua
Upper Hutt
Nelson
Hutt City
Wellington
Blenheim
Reefton
Rangiora
Leeston
Christchurch
Timaru
Cromwell
Alexandra
Oamaru
Dunedin
Invercargil

Notes

Chapter 3

1. George Otis, Jr., *Informed Intercession* (Ventura, Calif: Renew Books, 1999).
2. New Zealand Census 2001
3. Alcohol Advisory Council 2004
4. *The New Zealand Herald,* June 28, 2004
5. Michael King, *The Penguin History of New Zealand* (Penguin books, 2003).
6. *The New Zealand Herald,* Dec. 2, 2003

Chapter 6

1. Warner Hutchinson and Cliff Wilson, *Let the People Rejoice* (Wellington, New Zealand: Crusader Bookroom Society, 1959), 19.

Chapter 7

1. Mark 12:41-44
2. Acts 2:14-41
3. Jeremiah 23:29

Chapter 8

1. Nehemiah 1:4, Daniel 9:4-19
2. For an outline of how the Lord led Jim and Joy to intercede for New Zealand see Appendix A. I believe these principles could apply, with some modification, to any nation.
3. Private correspondence received from Joy Dawson, April 2004.
4. The Lydia Fellowship is an international prayer network mobilizing prayer cells of Christian women who intercede regularly with prayer and fasting for the church, community, country, and nations of the world. Contact details: lydiafellowship@maxnet.co.nz
5. Contributed by Joy Dawson

6. For further information contact Brian Caughley, Intercessors for New Zealand, PO Box 3399, Wellington, New Zealand; E-mail: ifnz@xtra.co.nz; Website: www.pray4thenation.org.nz

Chapter 9

1. See Appendix B for more details on counselor training.
2. 30,000 tracts printed, 30,000 *Real Life* New Testaments (special edition printed by The Bible Society of New Zealand).
3. Summary of main points of a message given by satellite by Joy Dawson to Revive Christchurch meeting, October 2003.
4. This story is told in Loren Cunningham, *Is That Really You, God?* (Seattle: YWAM publishing, 2001), 129ff.

Chapter 11

1. Weekly Updates were sent to members of executive task forces and those associated with IWT around the country.
2. Hutchison and Wilson, *Let the People Rejoice,* 133.
3. Ibid.
4. Eugene Petersen, *The Message* (Colorado Springs, Colo: NavPress, 2003).
5. Ten thousand copies of *Is That Really You, God?* were distributed at low cost for Impact World Tour in New Zealand.

Chapter 12

1. *The New Zealand Herald,* February 26, 2004
2. Thanks to Marlin Kroeger, TX member, for allowing us to use his diary of the tour.

Chapter 13

1. In 1973, Ralph Winter gave a landmark address to the All-Asia Mission Consultation in Seoul, Korea. His address was later published as "The Two Structures of God's Redemptive Mission" in Ralph Winter et al., *Perspective on the World Christian Movement: A Reader* (Pasadena: William Carey Library, 1981), 178-190.

Chapter 17

1. A quote from Joy Dawson given at Revive Christchurch, October 13, 2003.
2. *Ratu* is the title given to a Fijian chief.